VGM Careers for You Series

CAREERS FOR

SPORTS NUTS
& Other
Athletic Types

Second Edition

Wm. Ray Heitzmann

VGM Career Horizons
NTC/Contemporary Publishing Company

Library of Congress Cataloging-in-Publication Data

Heitzmann, William Ray.
    Careers for sports nuts & other athletic types / Wm. Ray Heitzmann
 ; foreword by Fred Hickman. — 2nd ed. / rev. by Mark C. Rowh.
      p.   cm. — (VGM careers for you series)
    ISBN 0-8442-4325-6 (cloth). — ISBN 0-8442-4514-3 (pbk.)
    1. Sports—Vocational guidance.   I. Rowh, Mark. II. Title.
 III. Series.
 GV734.H45   1997
 796'.023'73—dc21   97-14928
                                          CIP

Copyright © 1997 by NTC/Contemporary Publishing Company
Published by VGM Career Horizons
An imprint of NTC/Contemporary Publishing Company
4255 West Touhy Avenue, Lincolnwood (Chicago), Illinois 60646-1975 U.S.A.
Manufactured in the United States of America
International Standard Book Number: 0-8442-4325-6 (Hard); 0-8442-4514-3 (Soft)
15   14   13   12   11   10   9   8   7   6   5   4   3   2   1

Contents

About the Author

Ray Heitzmann has taught successfully in Pennsylvania, Illinois, and New York at the high school and college level. He served as a member of the adjunct faculty in the College of Allied Health Sciences at Thomas Jefferson University in Philadelphia. He received his Ph.D. from the University of Delaware.

A former successful athletic coach at the elementary, high school, and college level in New Jersey, Illinois, New York, and Pennsylvania, the author remains an avid student of the development and role of sports in society and performance enhancement of athletes. His coaching specialty features practice organization, strategy and techniques, and fundamentals development. Dr. Heitzmann has written several articles on sports and athletics; some have appeared in *Education Age, Coaching Clinic, Illinois Libraries, Catholic Library World, Coach and Athlete, The National Association of Basketball Coaches Bulletin, Career World, Philly Sport*, and others.

In the area of career education, he has authored articles for *Real World*, a career education newspaper for young people, and *Career World*, a career education magazine. His *Opportunities in Marine and Maritime Careers, Opportunities in Sports and Athletics*, and *Opportunities in Sports Medicine* have been published by VGM Career Horizons.

Active in professional organizations, he has received the National Council for the Social Studies Outstanding Service Award, has been named Outstanding Alumnus by the School of Education at the University of Delaware, and has received the MSCSS Gold Medal for outstanding research-based teaching publications.

Dr. Heitzmann speaks frequently at conferences, to high school and college groups, and on radio talk shows. He is the inventor of "Winner's Batter's Box."

Acknowledgments

The author would like to thank the many players, coaches, and associated people who have contributed to his love and knowledge of sports. In terms of this book, the author wishes to thank the following:

Ronnie Barnes, M.S., ATC
Mary Beilinske
Jack Bell
Jose Bernal
Don Casey
Kenneth Clarke, Ph.D.
James Clinkingbeard
Terry Conway
Jim Corea, Ph.D., R.P.T
Jerry Crawford
Joe Crawford
Stephanie Cugini
Donald Davidson
Ortho Davis
Vic D'Ascenzo
Jim Delorenzo
Vincent DiStefano, M.D.
Mary Edgerly

Page Elliott
William Emper, M.D.
Ronald Feingold, Ph.D.
Ann Fisher
Vincent Francia
Stephanie Gaitley
Stan Gallup
Joel Goodhart
Clara Gordon
Bucky Grace
Larry Hanzel
Karen Hargadon
Pat Harmon
Tom Harmon
Gerry Kaplan
I. Lawrence Kerr, D.D.S.
Ed Kershner
Barbara Kratchman

Kimberly Kumiega
Bob Lambert
Cathy Leonard
Janet Lippincott
Victor Livingston
Susan M. London
John Lumber
Barry Mano
Larry Mathews, Ed.D.
Philip J. Mayer, M.D.
Tim McCarver
Mike McClain
Mike McDyre
Andy McGovern
James McHugh
Joe McIlvanie
Peggy Kerschner McKernan
Bernard Meltzer
Ed Miersch, M.A., ATC
F. Don Miller
Heide Lee Morgan
Mike Moriarity
Pat Mosher, Ph.D.
Anne Moss
Andrew Myers, B.S., C.P.O.
Henry Nichols, Ed.D.
Stacie Nichols

Michael O'Shea
Shelley Pennefather
Richie Phillips
Millie Puccio
Ted Quedenfeld
Henry Reiter, Ph.D.
John Robinson
Jim Rohr
Gil Roman
Sam Rosenthal
Michael Sachs
Larry Schoppet
Larry Shane
Michele Sharp
Deena Shelton
Neal Sherman
Paul Smith
Dan Unger, ATC
Ron Valmassy, D.P.M.
Marty Walsh
D. Weight
Helen Welde
Harry Wendelstedt
Tim Whitaker
Jill White
Rick Wolff

A special thanks is made to Kathy, Rick, and Mary Heitzmann for their support as well as to Villanova University and to the Ragdale Foundation, Lake Forest, Ill., for their support during the preparation of the original manuscript. Thanks also goes to Mark Rowh, the talented and resourceful writer who revised this second edition.

A dedication is made to four basketball players I have had the privilege to coach who have passed away—Mike Dudick, North

Chicago High School (Illinois); Teddy Fikes, Highland Falls High School (New York); Ken Golder, Villanova University Nite Cats (Pennsylvania); and Brendon Kelly, Neumann College (Pennsylvania).

Foreword

I shall never forget that fall evening in 1972. I was a sophomore attending Springfield Southeast High in my hometown of Springfield, Illinois—the heart of what we considered to be the most fertile prep basketball cropland in America.

I was a player. I was not a great player, but I was on the roster. During those days, that alone was a sufficient magnet to capture the occasional coed's attention.

The problem was, I *wanted* to be a great player in the worst of ways. What a thrill it would be to play above the rim in Fighting Illini blue and orange as the crowd howled its approval. "Air Fred" shoes seemed a natural. Perhaps an MVP award or two along the way.

These were but some of the daydreams I was entertaining there at the far end of the bench when, for the first time in my basketball career, I was summoned by the coach to enter a contest.

At first, I thought it to be a rather cruel joke. After all, mine was the only uniform in SSHS history to have never required laundering. Why waste soap on something that wasn't soiled?

The reality of the situation finally seeped in. The warrior was being called to arms. I sprinted onto the floor, not realizing things such as removal of warm-ups and checking in with the scorer needed to be done first. These trivial impediments to my mission attended to, I hit the floor with a vengeance, wanting one thing and one thing only—I wanted to score. This was my chance. Perhaps my only chance. The entire Western world knew that the only way for a J-V player to get his name into the box score of the local paper was by scoring points. Fouls, assists, rebounds...none of those counted. Only the deuce.

Three quick fouls, each might have been punishable by 5 to 10 in the state pen had they been committed on the street.

Then, the jump ball. The tip went to my best friend, Leo Thompson. I flew out on the wing, crying, begging, pleading for the ball. Leo, swayed by the siren-sound of my calls, passed me the object of my desire and I put in one of the prettiest finger-roll layups you've ever seen.

But, why was there no cheering? Where was the adulation? This was my home court, and yet not one soul seemed to appreciate my effort.

For a moment, I thought I might have lost my hearing. That's when I saw that face, that nameless face in the second row. The one with what seemed to be two sets of teeth. The one crying...with laughter.

Fred Hickman, "Air Fred," had soared to and scored at the other team's basket.

It became clear to me at that moment in my life that I would never be a professional athlete. But, my dear love of sport continued to grow at a fever pace.

The only outlet I could find was sportscasting, and what a treasure it's been. Kind of like taking a trip without leaving the farm.

I have covered the big deals. The World Series. The Super Bowl. The NBA Finals. But I've also been blessed with seeing those magical midseason moments that are forgotten by those who were not there. Don Kessinger's inside-the-parker against the Pirates at Wrigley. Jim McMahon bringing the Bears back to beat the Vikings that Monday night.

The men and women I've met and the friendships I've made in this business are worth twice their weight in gold. Julius Erving. Satchell Paige. Gordie Howe. Michael Jordan. The list alone would make the casual fan green with envy and could easily fill several chapters of this work. My life has been enriched in count-less ways through my career in sports journalism. It has provided me with the vehicle to earn a better than decent living for my wife, Judith, and our family. It has allowed me to bring the fan the games through my eyes. Sports has allowed me to be a positive role model for other aspiring young black sports journalists, which is a tremendous honor.

Besides, nobody's had the guts to mention my scoring for the wrong team in years—an added plus. And, imagine, I've never once had to go on injured reserve or hold out or be traded for a sportscaster to be named later.

Yes, I enjoy the best of both worlds in this business of sports. Many others in different disciplines related to sports will tell you the same thing in the following pages.

Bet you never imagined the wide, wide world of sports could be *this* wide!

Fred Hickman
CNN Sports

Introduction

People love sports. From the great tradition of Canadian hockey to the excitement of baseball during spring training in Florida, people of all ages and backgrounds make sports a part of their lives.

Today, sports is show business. In many ways it's the fusing of business (often big business) and entertainment.

This sports phenomenon, which has become a religion for some and an obsession for others, may have a career for you. The jobs stretch from the coaches who shape athletic talent to the publicists who promote it.

An amazingly high level of job satisfaction categorizes this area, from the sports equipment salesperson selling bats and bowling balls to the agent insuring players and playing fields. June Hannah, wife of successful college baseball coach, Bob Hannah, nicely summarized the situation: "I don't mind the number of hours Bob spends with baseball. I'm just glad he is so happy with his career when so many people dislike their jobs."

The profession is likewise characterized by long hours of hard work and dedication. Bob Terry, retired championship wrestling coach at North Chicago High School, remarked that at one point during his coaching career, "I was working so many hours that I probably averaged a salary of 25 cents per hour!"

Outsiders often see only the glamour of sports careers—the limelight, big bucks, glory, and recognition. For every star who is a household name, there are a hundred laboring in the shadows. Even so, these unknowns (or locally knowns) love what they are doing.

This book should be read in its entirety because it explains the great interdependence among careers. For example, the successful football coach relies upon the ground crew, the sports information publicist, the statistician, the athletic trainer, and others. The successful minor league baseball team general manager relies upon the director of concessions, the marketing/sales manager, the sportswriters, the radio broadcasters, the team manager, among others. The reader will obtain an appreciation of these interrelations through a complete reading of the work.

The quickest route to obtaining a position in the field involves meshing an existing skill or specialty with sports. A lawyer could refocus toward becoming a sports agent. A nurse may take additional course work in athletic training to enter the profession. A computer specialist may wish to run the centerfield scoreboard, including "Fanavision," or tabulate sports statistics to discover trends and patterns. A dental technician might switch jobs to work with a dentist who caters to a sports clientele. A landscaper could design a baseball diamond. A radio announcer may specialize in broadcasting professional wrestling. An accountant might serve as a business manager for a college athletic department. Similarly, photographers, computer specialists, writers, and others can redirect their energies (sometimes with additional education) toward a self-fulfilling—and occasionally a lucrative—life in sports.

One ingredient remains a must for a sports career: interpersonal skills. Sports is a people business. You absolutely must be able to work with people, often under stress—losing streaks, deadlines, negotiations, game injuries, and budget inadequacies!

The ability to bring to sports experience and knowledge from another profession (or obtain the same through schooling) and couple it with people skills, a sense of humor, and a high energy level will result in a winning career. This refers not only to Max Plotkin, Crazy George, the Harlem Globetrotters, and the Chicken, but everyone!

The author hopes that this book will enhance the reader's understanding of the vast domain of sports careers and will assist you in entering that life resulting in personal and professional success, while contributing to a better world of sports.

CHAPTER ONE

Athletic Coaches

D o you love pressure? Like to make important decisions under the scrutiny of others? Then athletic coaching might be for you!

Professional Coaching

The prestige and salaries of professional coaches command everyone's attention. However, when their team loses regularly, they quickly become the victims of fans on radio sports talk shows and often commentators from the print and electronic media. Yet many love it and stay within the profession, despite poor job security, and even return following dismissal. This author has often theorized that the great highs and lows of the job at all levels must make it addictive.

The career of Don Casey, former coach of the National Basketball Association's Los Angeles Clippers, is typical of most who have made it to this lofty level. Coach Casey paid his dues at the high school level, culminating in his team, Bishop Eustace High School, winning the New Jersey state championship. He broke the record as the youngest coach to win the New Jersey championship; he was 22 at the time!

Coach Casey joined the basketball staff at Temple University following his tenure as a high school coach. First serving as an assistant coach and later as head coach, he continued to experience success. Prior to his service with the Clippers, he coached in Italy, at Notre Dame University, and as an assistant with the Chicago Bulls. Clearly the road to professional coaching is characterized by a difficult journey, but if you love your sport and love coaching, the bumps along the road will be felt less.

Lifestyles and Preparation

Most professional coaches have played the game they coach—many at the professional level. Depending on their visibility and popularity, some start their coaching careers as assistant coaches at the college or professional level. With success, they move to head coach status. Unfortunately, some move too quickly from player to head coach and amass a number of losses, quickly joining the ranks of the unemployed.

In addition to an intimate knowledge of the sport and extensive experience with it, professional-level head coaches need expert skills in dealing with players, the media, and fans. Likewise, they must motivate well-paid athletes to play hard and to continue to improve their skills. Often, head coaches have expert organizational skills as they juggle their exceptionally busy schedules, involving everything from luncheon presentations and talk show interviews to reviewing videotapes of previous games and evaluation of potential draft picks.

Assistant coaches' duties at this level vary greatly. Normally, they have a special expertise: for example, defensive end coach, strength and training coach, or pitching coach. Teams frequently have a number of specialists who work with the team in a consulting capacity: nutritionist, sports psychologist, exercise physiologist, and others.

Considerable hoopla surrounds professional sports teams, and no one can discount the glamour, the prestige, or the satisfaction of earned success. As with others in professional sports, coaches' salaries have escalated greatly, with head coaches of major sports often making more than $500,000 (sometimes more than $1 million) a year and assistant coaches exceeding $100,000. Media attention focuses no brighter anywhere in America than on winning professional coaches, nor does so little sympathy exist for a deposed loser. Fortunately, many of the skills necessary in coaching, such as organizational ability and skill in working with people, are useful in the business world. Consequently, most ex-pro coaches find employment in sales, public relations, and management. Others return to teaching while retaining an involvement in their sport by serving part-time as scouts. A fortunate few find careers as sports announcers.

The interest in sports shows no signs of slowing. There will be a continuing need for the few who make it to the select group designated as professional coaches.

The School Coach

Assistant Coach

The explosion of boys' and girls' sports in elementary, middle, and junior and senior high schools has created extensive opportunities for potential coaches. Many school athletic directors aggressively seek men and women to coach sports ranging from junior high girls' field hockey and softball to senior high boys' wrestling and football. They may even hire novices with little knowledge of the sport or of young people. The term *assistant coach* is used here to refer to all school coaches except the varsity head coach at the high school.

The ability to work with young people ranks as a major priority in selection of personnel. Intelligence and common sense plus some knowledge of the following will prove beneficial: first aid, legal issues related to coaching, practice organization, conditioning, motor skill development relative to the sport in question, coaching strategy, motivational techniques, and bench coaching. Additional knowledge in areas such as strength and fitness development, nutrition, or current developments in training and conditioning will aid any coach. Some school districts have excellent traditions of success in some sports and have dominated their regions and states. School administrators and the community carefully select and monitor even assistant coaches in their favored sport. Fierce competition for these positions would exist and the salaries would be above those of other sports. Typically, annual assistant coaching salaries range from $500 to $3,500. For instance, a middle school basketball coach may earn $1,200 and an assistant for varsity football may earn $3,000.

Do school coaches need to serve as physical educators or teachers in the schools at which they coach? At one time this was true, but it may not be today. Many schools utilize part-time coaches at all levels. These individuals have full-time jobs that permit them to coach practice in the late afternoon and participate in games on weekday afternoons and weekends. Usually these coaches love their sport and working with young people. They often attend workshops, clinics, and summer and off-season camps, as well as read and study games extensively to improve their skills and move to the next level.

Often it's the assistant coach who makes a major contribution to the development of young people, as players develop their love of a sport and build work habits and fundamental skills at the pre-varsity level. While a varsity coach may receive adulation or criticism for the team's performance, it's often the junior varsity coach who has made the difference.

Most coaches aspire to become a head coach. Following their successful apprenticeship as an assistant, they may move to the top position.

Head Coach

Rarely does the public know of the amount and variety of tasks performed by head coaches. A partial list of these activities follows:

- attending preseason workshops, clinics, and conferences for coaches
- taking inventory and ordering new equipment
- discussing scheduling with athletic director and opposing coaches
- arranging for preseason scrimmage games
- recruiting team managers and statisticians
- meeting regularly with assistant coaches
- making a schedule for scouting opponents
- announcing tryouts
- writing press releases for newspapers
- planning for use of athletic facilities
- clipping newspaper stories on the team and its opponents
- inviting the players' parents to the games
- monitoring players' academic progress
- asking knowledgeable persons to scout the team for weaknesses
- arranging for filming or videotaping of the team
- encouraging players to attend summer sports camp and participate in summer sports
- assisting players in their choice of colleges
- discussing the program and problems with the school principal and other administrators
- writing thank-you letters to appropriate individuals

If the above list looks like difficult work, you are correct; coaching is not easy. At the school level, few enter for financial reasons. Perhaps the numerous required duties lead many coaches to early retirement. It should be remembered that coaches have regular teaching duties to properly execute (such as class preparation, test correction, and course planning) as their primary obligation.

Because of turnover within coaching and the expansion of sports, many opportunities exist for coaching employment. Salaries vary with the emphasis the community places upon the sport, as well as local wage and salary practices. For example, a school district that regards football as very important may pay a coach $5,000 a season, while another district may pay $3,000. The average, according to the U.S. Department of Labor, is $2,000 to $4,000. Coaches of minor sports—tennis, wrestling, and swimming—may receive less than $1,000, unless there is strong local interest. Naturally, this is in addition to a teaching salary.

Also, many coaches at all levels in all sports direct summer camps or assist in such activities. This can be a welcome source of extra income.

At the school level, coaching, which is really an avocation, offers the opportunity to work closely with a group of young people and have a large impact upon their development. Many of the friendships made will be carried throughout the coach's life and provide a continuing source of satisfaction.

A coach can make a difference!

College Coaching

College coaching varies greatly with the visibility of the program and the status of the college or university. That is, a Division I (or IAA for football) program at a major university undoubtedly will have significant coverage of its games by the media and often have its games televised. This would not be true of Division II, III, or NAIA programs, although the latter would receive regular newspaper and periodic television coverage. So if you wish to be a superstar college coach on the television, aspire to Division I status. It's well to remember that many coaches greatly enjoy the small college and often achieve longevity there, far from the limelight.

Michele Sharp knew in high school that she wanted to coach basketball and perhaps some other sports. While enrolled at West Chester University in the health and physical education program, she served as an assistant coach in basketball and softball at nearby Cabrini College. Upon graduation, she gained employment as a health and physical education teacher and as a head coach in softball and basketball. Sharp remained active in the off-season through coaching Amateur Athletic Union (AAU) teams and working at summer basketball camps. Following successful stops at Philadelphia College of Textile and Science, Swarthmore College, and Norwich University, she now coaches at Manhattan College in Riverdale, New York.

"I love the players and enjoy the camaraderie of the coaches, and winning makes the hard work all worth it," she said, adding that she believes, "Opportunities for women in coaching abound. Although we don't have the extensive professional system men do, jobs are now available for women coaching men."

Volunteer Coaching

The opportunity of having a positive effect on young people is probably available in coaching more than in any other sports career. Nowhere is this truer than among volunteer coaches. Thousands of these coaches at all levels labor daily to develop their players to win games or events. The profession can be very rewarding, challenging, and self-fulfilling; but many days are hectic, tiring, and, unfortunately, thankless. Recently some coaches have openly expressed their disappointment in the lack of dedication of some athletes; that is, players who have sidetracked themselves—playing video games or "hanging out"—instead of committing themselves to self-improvement. Fortunately, the majority of athletes are more dedicated.

No one should coach unless he or she is familiar with and can implement "The Bill of Rights for Young Athletes." It serves as an excellent guideline for youth program coaches. Many of these rights should also be observed by coaches of high school and older players.

The Bill of Rights for Young Athletes

1. Right of the opportunity to participate in sports regardless of ability level.

2. Right to participate at a level that is commensurate with each child's development level.

3. Right to have qualified adult leadership.

4. Right to participate in safe, healthy environments.

5. Right of each child to share in the leadership and decision making of their sport participation.

6. Right to play as a child and not as an adult.

7. Right to proper preparation for participation in the sport.

8. Right to equal opportunity to strive for success.

9. Right to be treated with dignity by all involved.

10. Right to have fun through sport.

Many part-time and some full-time coaching situations exist for the interested volunteer; it's a wonderful entry into the profession. For those with a knowledge of their sport, an appreciation of children and young adults, and a desire to work daily to improve themselves, opportunities abound.

Most neighborhood, church, and community teams rely heavily upon volunteers to coach teams of young people. Little League Baseball, PAL, Pop Warner Football, YMCA, YMHA, YWCA, CYO, Optimist Youth Athletic programs, American

Legion Baseball, youth soccer leagues, and many similar groups could not serve the millions of players they do without the free services of many coaches. While some receive a salary, usually it is very little when the amount of time is considered. Yet, while the income may be none or little, the responsibility remains great—most often it is here that children receive their first experience with organized sports.

In recent years, it has become fashionable to criticize the abuses and mistakes of volunteer coaches. While some of this is clearly justified—a few coaches have overemphasized winning and underemphasized development of players and have poor practice organization—the vast majority of volunteer coaches make a substantial contribution.

Acting as a volunteer coach can serve as an enjoyable outlet while you benefit others. Unfortunately, many people take on the job with little information about the role and only superficial knowledge of the sport. In some cases, awkward situations and legal problems have occurred because of improper handling of behavior problems or an injury.

It is extremely important for any coach working with youngsters to prepare for the assignment. Experienced coaches realize that youngsters notice how a coach dresses and talks, handles emotion, uses fair standards, and knows the rules of the sport. They also understand that coaches can be held liable for any physical harm incurred by players in their charge.

Coaching is basically teaching, and good coaches build not only good athletes, but also good citizens.

Preparing to Coach

If you're planning a career as a coach, the time to begin is now.

The following abilities have been listed by the American Alliance for Health, Physical Education, Recreation, and Dance as necessary for the prospective coach. In preparing for your career, try to develop the following qualities:

- an understanding of the relationship of the interscholastic program and the particular sport you are coaching to the total education program
- a knowledge of first aid and the safety practices and techniques pertinent to the sport you are coaching
- an understanding of the possibilities of legal liability as well as sound practices and preventive measures
- a thorough knowledge and understanding of the biological, social, moral, emotional, and spiritual values that may accrue from the activity and the best methods of bringing about these desirable outcomes
- a knowledge of the most acceptable principles of growth and development and their implications for the sport
- an understanding of the basic principles in the care and prevention of injuries, together with an understanding of the proper relationship of the coach to the school or team physician
- an understanding of the best methods of developing and conditioning members of athletic squads
- the ability to speak in public to bring credit to the profession and the school and to more effectively inform the public of the educational possibilities of the sport
- an understanding of the basic psychological principles of motivation, stress, play, and group interaction
- a thorough knowledge of the fundamentals, offenses, defenses, strategies, and teaching methods involved in a particular sport (including squad organization, coaching techniques, and sound motivational procedures)
- a knowledge and sense of responsibility for local, state, and national rules

If you go to college to become a physical education teacher, you should achieve all of the above. People who either don't attend college or declare another major will need to prepare themselves.

This author offers the following suggestions for all those wishing to enter the ranks of the profession:

1. Begin reading and developing a library of books, articles, and clippings on coaching the sport of your interest. For example, a track coach should regularly read *Track Coach*, a quarterly journal covering techniques of this sport. Other publications worth reviewing include *Scholastic Coach and Athletic Director*, *Soccer Journal*, *Track and Field Coaches Review*, and *Canadian Journal for Health, Physical Education, Recreation, and Dance*. A number of fine videos also exist on both specific (Mike Fratello, *3-Point Strategy*) and general (Lou Holtz, *Changing Adversity into Opportunity*) topics.

2. Attend practices of several teams at various levels to observe coaches' organization and teaching techniques. This is important not only for nonathletes, but also for those who have participated in sports. It's easy to fall into the trap of coaching the way you were coached. Take the best and incorporate it into your system.

3. Observe as many games, matches, or meets as you can. While doing so, become a student of the sport. Observe how a coach performs magic or makes a mistake. For example, in basketball, how does the coach use time-outs? In hockey, how are substitutions handled? In football, what adjustments are made at halftime? In baseball, exactly when is a relief pitcher brought in to replace the starter? Quite often the difference between a fan and a person actually studying a game is that the fan watches only the main action (usually the ball), while the keen observer also watches the behavior of the other players and the actions of the coach.

4. Study the rules and rule changes of your sport so that as coach, you will be knowledgeable in using the rules for your benefit and that of your team. Strategy frequently revolves

around the rules of the game, with opposing coaches working to gain an advantage.

5. Select some coaches whom you admire and use them as role models for yourself. You may want to write and ask them to share some of their materials with you. Many coaches will provide information on their approaches to the sport, including specifics in areas such as practice organization and weight training. A coaching model need not have a fantastic record; many coaches are very good, yet have only mediocre win-loss histories.

6. Discover what functions sports officials, scorekeepers, statisticians, and athletic directors perform at an athletic event. If you do not have athletic ability, you may wish to volunteer to serve as a manager or statistician for a team. One of the best ways to gain an excellent close-up feel for athletics is to serve as a referee, judge, or umpire. Not only does this enable you to practice instant recall of the rules, but you also gain an insight into the flow of the event. Frequently, lower-level sports teams go begging for officials. Volunteer—*it will make you a better coach*.

7. Investigate the off-season techniques to develop players in your sport. For example, weight training equipment and procedures, conditioning, and nutrition have changed dramatically in recent years. Future coaches should stay informed about these developments. Observe athletes and their coaches in working situations during the off-season.

8. Attend professional meetings, conferences, and clinics, and join the coaching associations related to your sports interest. Membership in the following organizations is strongly encouraged:

National Youth Sports Coaches Association
2050 Vista Parkway
West Palm Beach, FL 33411-2718

National High School Athletic Coaches Association
P.O. Box 5020
Winter Park, FL 32793-5020

Coaching Association of Canada
1600 James Naismith Drive
Gloucester, Ontario Canada K1B 5N4

National Federation
Interscholastic Coaches Association
P.O. Box 20626
Kansas City, MO 64195

9. Participate in sports. If you are able to compete at the varsity level, play on intramural and community teams.

10. Volunteer to serve as an assistant coach for a team of children in your community. This will give you the experience as well as the opportunity to learn and experiment in developing your own coaching system and philosophy.

Coaching can be one of the most positive and wholesome careers our society has to offer. In order to realize these benefits, a tremendous commitment of time and energy will be needed—and the earlier you begin, the better. If you think it may not be worth it, consider the following excerpt from an article entitled "Thoughts about My Coach," from the magazine *Young Athlete*:

Back in the early 1920s, when I was in the seventh grade at West Orange, New Jersey's Fairmount Middle School, I met a man who changed my whole life.

His name was Lawrence Quallo, our athletic director.... As a youngster I was not a very good athlete, but I did my best. Then one day on the basketball court, after I had been lucky enough to score, Mr. Quallo stopped the game, came over to me and asked, "Eddie, would you like to try out for our team?... I think you have the makings of a good player."

Thanks to Larry Quallo's influence, I went on to become a fairly good three-letter man in high school. So much did Larry inspire and guide me that, when I was in my junior year of high school, I scored over 1,000 points for the basketball team (I missed only one foul shot), scored 11 touchdowns and ran the hundred in 10 seconds flat. I tried to please Larry. My reward? He said he was more than pleased. That was enough . . .

I'm now in the Hall of Fame, but only because of Larry. He helped my dreams come true. He put a real foundation under my dreams, insuring they'd become reality. He was like a father to me, and I bless his memory every day of my life.

CHAPTER TWO

Sports Managers and Administrators

T he explosive interest in anything "sports" is clearly reflected in the realm of sports management and adminis-tration. Careers range from director of marketing and pro-motions, through assistant general manager and school athletic director, to vice president for operations.

Professional Team Positions

These careers not only include those with major league teams, but also the numerous opportunities available with minor league affiliates. Jim Rohr, speaking of his experience as assistant general manager of the Toledo Mud Hens, a Detroit Tigers baseball minor league affiliate, exclaimed, "I love it! I love all aspects of the job, but particularly the people—the fans, the players, the staffs from opposing teams . . ." The job includes managing sales, public rela-tions, and marketing for the Hens, which average approximately 3,000 fans a game. "This business is difficult to get into—there is very little turnover—but be persistent," Rohr suggested.

If you think working a minor league team lacks electricity and excitement, think again. The players play hard, the management works hard, and the fans cheer hard. Even Chicken Man makes the rounds of the parks. The following is a list of the many jobs associated with the Richmond Braves, a minor league affiliate of the Atlanta Braves baseball team:

General manager

Associate general manager

Office manager/Executive secretary

Field maintenance director

Director of stadium operation

Director of ticket operations

Assistant ticket manager

Administrative assistants

Receptionist

Home club house manager

Associate home club house manager

Visiting club house manager

Umpire room manager

Radio announcers

Official scorer

Public address announcer

Message center operator

Scoreboard operator

Organists

The conclusion: the minor leagues *are* big time!

The question: "How does someone obtain employment in this field?"

Currently the preferred route lies through participation in a college program in sports management. A number exist; the following typify contemporary programs. St. Thomas University in Miami, Florida, became one of the first institutions to offer a Master of Science in Sports Administration. The program prepares students for careers in professional, college, and community sports business as well as careers in the management of sports facilities. Graduates have entered a variety of careers—traveling secretary, Houston Astros; athletic fund raiser, University of Houston; assistant executive director, the Orange Bowl; sports information director, University of Tulsa; assistant public relations director, Los Angeles Rams; and arena manager, Yates Field House, Georgetown University.

Courses at St. Thomas include "Seminar on ethics in sports administration," "Principles of sports administration," "Legal aspects of sports administration," "Sports financial management," and others. A major aspect of all such programs is the internship— a chance to work in the sports industry (sometimes paid) as an apprentice. St. Thomas interns have worked for the New York Knicks, the U.S. Olympic Committee, the National Football League Office, Hialeah Race Track, Kansas City Parks and Recreation, the Nashua (New Hampshire) Pirates, and many others.

Georgia State University offers a Master of Science degree in Sports Administration. The program requires a core of courses; for example, "Sports law," "Sports marketing and promotion," "Cultural aspects of sports," "Budgeting and finance in sports and recreation," and "Governance and ethical issues in sports." In addition, students may take electives in a variety of related subjects.

Karen Hargadon typifies students in such programs. A basketball player in high school and college, she wished to continue her interest in sports. She obtained a graduate assistantship at the University of Richmond under successful basketball coach Stephanie

Gaitley. She enrolled in a master's degree program in sports management and, following course work and successful internship with the Philadelphia 76'ers NBA basketball team, she graduated. She then landed a job in sports promotions for Trump Castle and Casino, publicizing everything from boxing and professional wrestling to one-on-one basketball contests.

Most of today's upper-level managers have their college training in management or law. For example, Stan Kastan, president of the Atlanta Braves and the Atlanta Hawks, received his undergraduate degree in psychology and graduate degree in law. However, other managers have had backgrounds ranging from attending business schools to religious seminaries. Clearly, there are many paths to leadership positions. But the majority of future leaders will have a college background in sports management.

School and College Administrators

Gerry Kaplan, former athletic director (AD) at O'Neil High School in Highland Falls, N.Y., in many ways typified a successful sports administrator. He started out as a basketball coach and physical education teacher. Upon the retirement of the previous AD, he was appointed by the board of education to the position of athletic director. In addition to his teaching duties as physical educator, he coached the varsity basketball team. He taught his classes in the early part of the day, leaving the afternoon free for administrative duties—scheduling, attending meetings, coordinating intramurals, and other matters. At smaller schools, the AD may teach several classes; at larger schools, the position may command full-time attention. Hiring, evaluating, and terminating coaches requires many hours in this era of expansion of high school and college interscholastic athletics. Consider also the rainy afternoon when you have to cancel baseball and softball games, a track meet, and a tennis match—then call and notify the games' officials and the bus company to reschedule!

If this sounds demanding, consider the athletic director at the University of Texas who lists under his jurisdiction the following areas: business office (tickets, concessions); sports information; trainers and equipment manager; coaches; athletic dining hall; and stadium supervision. The Texas AD has assistant and secretarial support; this is common at the major universities. The position varies with the size of the school or college. Recently, many colleges (and some high schools) have added a director or coordinator of women's athletics. And don't overlook the growing opportunities afforded by the community college.

Salaries average in the range of $25,000 to $70,000 a year according to the U.S. Department of Labor, although some AD's earn more. The salary is often for twelve months of work, as opposed to the ten-month time commitment of teachers.

According to the College and University Personnel Association, average salaries for athletic directors in U.S. colleges and universities range from $48,000 to more than $101,000 annually, depending on the size and type of institution. The higher figures are earned by athletic directors at large universities with prominent sports programs.

College athletic directors' functions vary with the size of the college and the athletic program. At small (NCAA division III and NAIA division II) colleges, they function much like their high school counterparts, and at tiny colleges, they may operate only on a part-time basis. However, NCAA Division I is most often big time—television contracts, game guarantees, major arenas, and stadiums, and increased pressure to win. At this level, the AD will have a staff of associates and assistants as well as business managers and publicists. Frequently working very long hours, these individuals—some with six figure salaries—attend many meetings and games; approve contracts; hire and fire; keep the peace among coaches; meet with players, fans, faculty, and alumni; and generally serve as commander-in-chief. At Yale University, for example, the associate athletic director performs many functions—one even involves proper and humane burial of horses! (Yale has an equestrian team.)

Some professional organizations list the abilities necessary in athletic administrators. These include an understanding of:

- the role of athletics in education and our society and the rules, regulations, policies, and procedures of the various governing bodies
- sound business procedures as related to athletic administration
- administrative problems as related to athletic equipment and supplies administration
- problems related to facilities, both indoor and outdoor
- school law and liability
- the factors involved in the conduct of athletic events
- good public relations techniques
- staff relationships
- the health aspects of athletics
- the psychological and sociological aspects of sports

Often important personality qualities include:

- leadership
- a sincere interest in young people and their development
- a sense of humor
- even temperament
- optimism
- a sense of justice and impartiality
- integrity and solidarity

Some ADs at all levels enter their profession with college-level training in sports management; most, however, are products of physical education administration programs. Montclair State University in New Jersey offers such a graduate program. Students may concentrate on teaching and administration of physical education, coaching and sports administration, or exercise sciences. They take courses in "Administration and supervision of athletics and coaching," "Applied sport psychology," "Orientation to sports medicine," and others. College programs vary, including some with similar titles. For example, the sports administration specialty in the physical education master's program at Indiana State University has more of a public relations emphasis. It involves an internship and requires two elective courses outside the program. It does include the courses "Public relations in physical education and athletics," "Physical education and the law," and "Social psychological aspects of sports." Exciting, cutting-edge courses such as those at MSU and ISU make an important contribution to future administrators.

Park and Recreation Managers

Another specialty within sports administration worthy of consideration is park and recreation management. Arkansas Tech University explains its undergraduate programs:

- *Recreation Administration*—prepares students to work in community agency settings and commercial recreation business. Programming and people management are major areas of expertise.
- *Park Administration*—prepares students to manage large resource areas and visitor facilities. Planning and management aspects of land and water are taught, with private and public recreation and park system as targeted work careers.

Both of these fine programs feature a wide array of courses and an internship.

A specialty in this area can be obtained in colleges at the graduate level. For example, the University of Rhode Island, within the Master of Science in Physical Education program offers a specialty in Sports and Recreation Management and Recreation Education. Students pursue course work in "Current issues in physical education, health, and recreation operations," "Sports and recreation," "Principles of recreation leadership," and others.

Sports management is fun, and it's growing, but it also is hard. Not sure if its for you? Do what Gil Roman did. He served as the part-time business manager for athletics at Jersey City State College while completing his degree in business. All sports programs have business managers. For some, the job is mainly bookkeeping, collecting, and paying the bills. For others, a wider variety of duties are performed by a considerable staff. Regardless, it's a good way to break into the field and/or assess the situation.

CHAPTER THREE

Fitness Careers

An explosion of interest in physical fitness has taken place in recent years. Well-informed people have learned that overall good health and longevity are directly related to cardiopulmonary conditioning, weight control, and muscular strength and flexibility. The desire to look marvelous, feel good, and live to a "ripe old age" has resulted in a major boom for the fitness industry.

This fitness boom has resulted in the expansion of opportunities for careers in the following industries: health clubs, sporting goods (such as sneakers and clothing), specialized equipment (including weight-training equipment of all varieties), "natural" food, vitamins, minerals, herbs, fitness videos, medical/health radio talk shows, relaxation equipment, and related products.

Fitness

Physical fitness takes many forms. While there is some debate over aspects of conditioning and training, most experts agree on the main emphases—weight training, endurance, agility, stretching and running for speed, and cardiovascular strength.

Several studies have examined various sports in terms of their contribution to fitness (and, of course, each sport's demands upon the player). Based upon a 1–10 system, the following list rates various sports according to muscle, lung, and heart requirements.

Auto racing	3		Ice hockey	7
Baseball	3		Judo	7
Basketball	8		Lacrosse	6
Bicycling	4		Marathon	9
Boxing	9		Paddleball	4
Cross-country	6		Relay racing	6
Decathlon	10		Rodeo	3
Field hockey	6		Scuba diving	3
Football	7		Swimming	6
Handball	8		Weight lifting	4

The President's Council on Physical Fitness has developed a similar rating system, using a scale of 0–21, as shown in the following chart.

	Jogging	Swimming	Basketball	Tennis	Calisthenics	Golf	Bowling
Cardio-respiratory (endurance; stamina)	21	21	19	16	10	8	5
Muscular endurance	20	20	17	16	13	8	5
Muscular strength	17	14	15	14	16	9	5
Flexibility	9	15	13	14	19	8	7
Balance	17	12	16	16	15	8	6
Weight control	21	15	19	16	16	6	5
Muscle definition	14	14	14	13	18	6	5
Digestion	13	13	10	12	11	7	7
Sleep	16	16	12	11	12	6	6

This chart provides information on how demanding the sport(s) of your choice will be, and your training should follow accordingly. Be sure to include a program of flexibility; increased availability of training equipment in recent years has created a sensation in this regard. Likewise, stretching has become part of everyone's program to avoid injury.

The trend toward aerobic exercise continues to gain momentum. Aerobic exercises challenge the heart, lungs, and muscles to become stronger and more efficient at the delivery and utilization of oxygen. Aerobic exercise thus makes all of these organs stronger and healthier. In practice, the aerobic exercises utilize the large muscle groups in a repetitive fashion. Common types of aerobic exercise in health clubs include stationary cycling, stair climbing, stationary rowing, walking, jogging, swimming, cross-country skiing, and aerobic dance.

Research indicates that when done properly, aerobic activity yields the following positive results:

- promotes strong and healthy bones
- controls the physical and emotional stress in your life
- improves your intellectual capacity and increases your productivity
- helps you to lose fat and keep it off
- provides significant protection from heart disease
- achieves maximum benefits in a minimum amount of time

"Paying the price," long a slogan in sports, has no greater application than in the area of physical conditioning and training. For some, the price is too great unless looked upon in a positive fashion. That is, the process can be as enjoyable as the result—looking good, feeling good, and living longer and better.

Health Clubs

Following attendance at San Antonio Community College and Cisco Community College in Texas, Jose Bernal found himself

behind a computer in an 8-to-5 job. Obtaining a transfer, he found improved job satisfaction as a sales representative, largely because he liked working with people. However, not until he joined the staff of President's Health Club in Plano, Texas, did he truly enjoy his career while teaching aerobics and serving as the club's service manager.

"I enjoy the real cross section of society that our club attracts, and I like working with people to improve their health," said Bernal. His teaching has included abdominal aerobics, calisthenics, dance, stretching, and a hips-and-thighs routine. Bernal suggested that if you plan to consider his type of career, "you must have a positive personality, be a motivator, and thoroughly like people."

Not all aerobic instructors work full-time. Steph Cugini served part-time at Buena Athletic Club in New Jersey while attending college full-time.

"I love aerobics—it gives me a chance to work out, to teach, and I get paid!" she exclaimed. Cugini obtained her certification during a demanding three-day weekend workshop involving evaluation of her knowledge, skills, and teaching effectiveness. The Aerobics and Fitness Association of America organized and conducted the course.

The skill and knowledge of the club employee is critical to the health of the client. Well-trained instructors will provide advice to help avoid injury and maximize the benefits of the workout. They also help motivate people to improve their levels of fitness.

Health clubs exist in a variety of geographic settings. The neighborhood mall and the city club are the most common, but others may be in retirement communities, aboard cruise ships, or in large motels and hotels. Corporate fitness/health clubs have also become common.

Within this variety, clubs range from the very serious (very expensive)—emphasizing testing and medical evaluation, with specialized programs and rehabilitation, if necessary—to those simply featuring weight-training equipment and aerobic exercise. Accordingly, careers range greatly, from those requiring extensive knowledge and education to those requiring little. Naturally, salaries also vary greatly.

Administrative personnel in the health club industry mirror those of many other commercial enterprises. The major national and regional clubs have assistant managers, a manager, and a regional/district supervisor—and, for national organizations, an executive staff. Independent clubs exist with administrative personnel just for the single club. These single clubs vary greatly in quality; some are excellent, while others are poor and consequently often fail to survive financially.

At the club level, administrative personnel perform many of the functions of typical service-related industries. They plan budgets; arrange work schedules; hire, evaluate and dismiss personnel; supervise the maintenance of equipment and wet areas (whirlpool, steam rooms, pool); plan sales quotas; and perform other similar tasks.

In most health clubs, all employees except some specialists have the responsibility to sell memberships. Their job performance is rated to a large degree on this basis. Additionally, sales commissions form an important part of their salary. Consequently, health club personnel must have excellent sales skills as well as an in-depth knowledge of fitness and conditioning.

Corporate Health Clubs

As with commercial health clubs, their corporate counterparts vary widely in sophistication. Some may offer their employees merely a swimming pool or volleyball/basketball courts and a shower facility, while others have the capability of providing medical testing of one's fitness, conducting a monitored program for improvement, and offering education programs such as smoking cessation or relaxation therapy. The trend in the industry leans toward the latter center. Naturally, there is no charge to corporate employees for health club membership, so club workers do not have to sell memberships. If sales is not your thing, this may be a more viable career option.

Corporate fitness centers represent a recent and expanding trend on the health scene. As more enlightened managers and labor leaders realize its value to people and the company, they will include it in collective bargaining agreements for nonmanagerial personnel, as a perk for their executives, and generally as a recruiting tool for prospective employees. Hence, job prospects with corporate health clubs will prove very good.

Exercise physiologists often are hired to manage these facilities. Dr. Ron Feingold, professor of the Department of Physical Education and Human Performance Science at Adelphi University on Long Island, New York, reports that Adelphi's graduate program in exercise physiology has shown excellent growth, attracting students with backgrounds in physical education, nursing, physical therapy, and related areas who all wish to move into this exciting new area.

Some sports medicine centers, such as those associated with hospitals, offer wellness programs to the public. These feature supervised fitness and educational programs similar to corporate centers and require participation fees.

Education

Most health club managers have college backgrounds in physical education, exercise physiology, or sports science. For corporate centers, a college degree in a fitness speciality is a must. Obviously, if the club features extensive fitness testing, specialists including medical personnel will be necessary. However, most employees do not need to have a college education, but acquire the training and knowledge that many people obtain on the job or certification received through a professional organization.

Naturally, appearance remains vital to hiring and retention; you must not only be able to play the part, but also *look* the part. Perhaps someday you will receive an invitation to join the prestigious National Fitness Leaders Association and follow the paths of fitness leaders such as Joe Weider, Denise Austin, Richard Simmons, Jack LaLanne, Joannie Greggains, Cory Everson, and others.

For Further Reading

The following organizations provide information relative to fitness careers:

Areobics and Fitness Association of America
15250 Ventura Boulevard, Suite 200
Sherman Oaks, CA 91403-3297

International Association of Fitness Professionals
6190 Cornerstone Court East, Suite 204
San Diego, CA 92121-4701

American Association for Active Lifestyles and Fitness
1900 Association Drive
Weston, VA 22091-1599

Associated Bodywork and Massage Professionals
28677 Buffalo Park Road
Evergreen, CO 80439-7347

International Sports Sciences Association
1035 Santa Barbara Street
Santa Barbara, CA 93101

African-American Association of Fitness Professionals
1507 E. 53rd Street
Chicago, IL 60615

Association for Worksite Health Promotion
60 Revere Drive, Suite 500
Northbrook, IL 60062

National Fitness Foundation
2250 E. Imperial Highway, Suite 412
El Segundo, CA 90245

National Fitness Leaders Association
7929 Westpark Drive
McLean, VA 22102

American Council on Exercise
5820 Oberlin Drive
San Diego, CA 92121-8227

CHAPTER FOUR

Sports Officials

Without skilled umpires, I knew, the game could not exist. Oh, players were important, I accepted that, but there were plenty of players—too many players as far as some umpires were concerned. But there were only a select few people with the knowledge and judgment required to control a major league game.

RON LUCIANO
Former Major League Umpire, in *The Fall of the Roman Umpire*

Officials: they were once the quiet people of sports. Now they write books, appear on radio and TV talk shows, show militancy, have name recognition among fans, take superiors and coaches to court, do commercial advertising in print and electronic media—they have joined show business.

Ninety-five percent of all officials serve on a part-time basis, working mostly with schools and colleges, but also with semiprofessional teams and recreational leagues. Most feel like Peggy Kershner McKernan, one of the first women to officiate boys' high school basketball, who said, "I love it. It works well with my lifestyle and family obligations, and I enjoy the physical activity and the income it provides."

For many years, officiating was considered a thankless job in which the official took verbal abuse—and occasionally physical abuse—from the coach, players, and crowd. More recently, a growing respect has been noticeable at all levels for the men and women who make the game work by enforcing the rules. This probably has occurred because of growing militancy on the part of the officials, an increase in their skills, and a realization of their importance and dedication by the public. However, a growing feeling exists by many students of sports that perhaps officials should return to a less visible role.

Marty Walsh is typical of those who work as officials on a part-time basis.

"My officiating background in both football and baseball has been filled with both exciting and rewarding experiences," Walsh commented. He attended the University of Delaware, playing football and baseball, and graduating with a major in biology. During his officiating career in Delaware, Maryland, New Jersey, Pennsylvania, North Carolina, and Virginia, he quickly moved up the ladder. He has officiated numerous championship high school football games and worked many NCAA-IAA college football games; in baseball, he has "umped" high school and college playoff and championship assignments and some minor league professional games. Active in officials' associations, he has served in numerous professional capacities. Noted Walsh, "I feel the friendships I've developed and my professional growth are invaluable by-products of this avocation."

The schedule of the official is not for everyone. Weekdays see them scurrying from their full-time positions to contests; weekends, likewise, prove hectic as the officials work games on Saturdays and, in some leagues, even on Sundays!

Many officials earn their livelihood as educators. Others own their own businesses or work flexible hours in careers such as sales so as to be available for afternoon sporting events.

While most view the profession as an avocation, a select few make it to the inner circle of full-time professional officials. These individuals normally pay their dues as did Marty Walsh: by obtaining several years of experience at the lower levels, such as high school, college, and the minor leagues.

Richie Powers, in his classic book *Overtime* (Ballantine), provided an excellent look at the life of a professional basketball official in the National Basketball Association. He stated:

> "I'm usually quick with the whistle and even quicker with my thumb, in the area of technical fouls, but I set a record tonight by calling my first technical of the season less than two minutes into the game. Manny (Sokol) had called a foul against Phil Chenier of the Bullets. Instead of rolling the ball to Manny, or at least bouncing it toward him, Chenier held it defiantly, glaring in Manny's direction. Then he flipped the ball out of bounds. Tweet! I hit him with a technical foul for unsportsmanlike conduct…Listen, I call technical fouls in an attempt to maintain control of the game."

Quite obviously, the emotional control of officials is tested many times in each game.

Officiating Guidelines

The following guidelines (almost requirements) have been prepared by *Referee* magazine for officials:

- *Be competitive*—The players give maximum effort, and so should you. Tell yourself, "I'm not going to let this game get away from me, I am better than that." You are hired to make the calls that control the game—make them!
- *Have your head on right*—Don't think your striped shirt grants you immunity from having to take a little criticism. It's part of officiating. Plan on it. Successful officials know how much to take. Ask one when you get the chance.
- *Don't be a tough guy*—If a coach is on your back, but not enough to warrant a penalty, then stay away from him (or her). This is especially true during time-outs. Standing near an unhappy coach just to "show him" will only lead to further tensions. Some officials develop irritating characteristics. Don't be one of them.

- *Get into the flow of the game*—Each game is different. Good officials can feel this difference. Concentrate on the reactions of
  the players. Take note if the tempo of the game changes. A
  ragged game calls for a different style of officiating than a
  smooth one.
- *Don't bark*—If you don't like to be shouted at, don't shout at
  someone else. Be firm, but speak with a normal, relaxed voice.
  This technique will do wonders in helping you reduce the pressure. Shouting indicates a loss of control, not only of one's self,
  but also of the game.
- *Show confidence*—Cockiness has absolutely no place in officiating. You want to exude confidence. Your presence should command respect from the participants. As in any walk of life,
  appearance, manner, and voice determine how you are
  accepted. Try to present the proper image.
- *Forget the fans*—As a group, fans exhibit three common characteristics: (1) ignorance of the rules, (2) highly emotional parti-
  sanship, and (3) delight in antagonizing the officials. Accepting
  this fact will help you ignore the fans, unless they interrupt the
  game or stand in the way of your doing your job.
- *Answer reasonable questions*—Treat coaches and players in a
  courteous way. If they ask you a question reasonably, answer
  them in a polite way. If they get your ear by say "Hey, Ref, I
  want to ask you something," and then start telling you off,
  interrupt and remind them of the reason for the discussion. Be
  firm, but relaxed.
- *Choose your words wisely*—Don't aggressively threaten coaches
  or players. This will only put them on the defensive. More
  important, you will have placed yourself on the spot. If you feel
  a situation is serious enough to warrant a threat, then it is serious enough to penalize, without invoking a threat. Obviously
  some things you say will be a form of threat, but using the
  proper words can make it subtle.
- *Stay cool*—Your purpose is to establish a calm environment for
  the game. Nervous or edgy officials are easily spotted by fans,

coaches, and players alike. Avoid chewing gum, pacing around, or displaying a wide range of emotions prior to or during a game; this will make you seem vulnerable to the pressure.

The above suggestions, generally applicable to officiating at all levels, may need slight modification in special situations. However, as a whole, they provide useful guidelines. Excellent mechanics and a thorough knowledge of the rules are an important part of being a truly successful official. But establishing and maintaining rapport with coaches and players also will help the official avoid many potentially difficult situations.

One researcher, Dr. Roy Askins, a professor of social psychology with officiating experience, examined his hobby and provided the following information. When asked, "What gives officials the most trouble?" Dr. Askins replied that other than problems associated with perception and sloppy plays, the behavior of some coaches, players, and crowds is most troublesome.

At this point, you may ask, "If officiating is so demanding in terms of working conditions, why do people do it?" A survey administered by Dr. Askins found many reasons. The most common were: earning extra money, remaining close to athletics in some capacity, and enjoying a position of some status and power. If you think this career looks promising for you, make plans to begin.

Getting Started

What kind of person makes a good sports official? Dr. R. C. Haygood, a vocational psychologist at Arizona State University, said that the ideal sports official is a saint, for only a saint could exhibit all of the psychological traits we expect of a good referee or umpire! Some of these personality characteristics are tolerance, self-confidence, and the ability to make decisions under stress. There's one way to see if you possess these: give officiating a try.

If you're interested, volunteer to officiate in a youth summer league, in a church or synagogue league in your neighborhood, or in the community recreation program. Many league officers at this level go begging for officials! Your involvement can aid both yourself and the league; some youth leagues and intramural programs even provide salaries, but your greatest benefit will be experience. In addition, officiating is an excellent way to better understand a sport; it will give you a greater appreciation of the total game as well as a working knowledge of the rules. This serves as a valuable background for related careers.

If you become seriously interested, it's useful to remember that officiating parallels coaching in many respects. That is, novices work with younger players at the lower level. So, following approval, you usually will work games at the junior high school and junior varsity levels. In order to receive initial status, it will be necessary to pass a written examination in the sport or sports of your choice and to join the state officials' association as well as the local chapter.

During the probationary period, usually a couple of years, the newcomer will come under the observation of senior officials for evaluation. They will look for a good working knowledge of the game, combined with several abilities—for example, how well he or she performs in a stressful situation. As new officials improve their skills, they will be asked to work more games and be promoted to higher-level games, perhaps even an important tournament or championship event. Naturally, salaries improve with the level officiated. They also vary with geographic location.

Some officials will want to move on to the college level. This will involve joining another association, taking a test, and proving oneself again. College officials receive very good per-game salaries, and most conferences also pay travel expenses.

One major college conference listed its requirements: applicants for officials' positions should be less than forty years of age when applying, in good physical condition, and able to pass an exam. These requirements must be met, and three ability references must be submitted. While a high school diploma is necessary, a college degree is preferred. In addition, the person must have employment and residence in close proximity to the conference. The candidate's job has to permit flexibility so the official is free for travel and games. While some background as a player is desirable, the officiating experience must include eight to ten years at the high school level plus approximately four years in a comparable conference. If these criteria appear too demanding, remember that most positions will not be this difficult to obtain—the above requirements represent a special situation for one of the nation's premier conferences.

Officiating Schools

Although a study of the readership of *Referee* magazine indicated that most officials became introduced to their profession by a friend or through participation in sports, many future officials probably will enter their career as a result of attendance at a school. The officials' associations provide a training program for their new recruits; the schools, however, represent an in-depth, concentrated approach to learning the officials' art. Some master officials conduct annual conferences for officials. These clinics, usually two-day meetings, exist for officials of all levels who wish to improve their skills.

The following serve as typical examples of the schools available. One of the nation's best-known and most popular programs is the Harry Wendelstedt School for Umpires. The specific purpose is to supply supervised training for young people to qualify for umpire positions in professional, college, high school, semi-pro, and sandlot baseball. The school, which meets for six weeks, runs from directly after the New Year's holiday until early February. The program follows this schedule. Classes begin at 8:30 A.M. with a ninety-minute session that explains and tests the student's knowledge of the rules and situations that actually confront umpires. At 10:30 A.M., the class reports to the playing fields, where a program of exercises and conditioning takes place. Following this, a series of practice drills provides instruction in proper mechanics—stance, voice control, positions, and others. Each student receives instruction and practice in all phases of umpiring. After the completion of the first ten days of school, the late afternoons—3:30 P.M. until 6:00 P.M.—are spent working high school and college games.

No jobs are promised, but many of Wendelstedt's graduates have entered the profession at all levels. Some (approximately 15) exceptional students do receive appointments directly after finishing the school, and many are called at a later date. This school has trained the majority of the officials in blue working in the majors today. If this sounds interesting, for additional information write:

Harry Wendelstedt School for Umpires
88 S. Street Andrews Drive
Ormond Beach, FL 32174

One graduate, Ed Barycki, decided to attend the school after working a few softball games: "The umpiring bug bit me, and I went to Harry's just wanting to learn, and I ended up the top graduate in the class!" Following graduation, Barycki worked in the South Atlantic League, then in the Carolina League (both affiliates of major league baseball). However, he missed the time away from his home and family. He gave up his attempt to make it to the "bigs." However, he stayed within the profession by moonlighting as an umpire for major college games on the East Coast.

Other schools for umpires include:

Brinkman-Froemming Umpire School
1021 Indian River Drive
Cocoa, FL 39222

Jim Evans Academy of Professional Umpiring
12885 Research Boulevard
Austin, TX 78750

Eric Gregg, in his book *Working the Plate: The Eric Gregg Story,*
suggested that umpires in the minors not marry—they cannot
afford it. Salaries for umpires in these leagues remain very poor.
(Undoubtedly, this contributed to Ed Barycki's decision to give
up the minor league life.) According to the Major League Baseball Umpire Development Program, salaries for minor league
umpires ranged from $2,000 to $3,400 per month in 1997.

Typical subjects covered by student umpires include:

- in-depth examination of the current Official Baseball Rule
  Book
- homeplate mechanics, including timing, voice control, and
  positioning
- instruction in moral conduct
- proper use of fair and foul signals by base and home-plate
  umpires
- extensive use of video aids
- guest lectures
- practice, practice, practice of umpiring skills

Each summer, Nationwide Basketball Referee's Camp hosts
many active and aspiring officials. In 1997, sessions were held at
the University of South Carolina in Columbia, South Carolina,
and the University of Tennessee in Knoxville. The three-day sessions attract people from all over the country. The camp format
begins with morning presentations, films, and lectures. Topics
such as "Floor mechanics," "What type of officials supervisors
look for at the higher levels," "Personality traits of successful officials," and "Proper use of signals" form some of the content of the
course.

Following lunch, the refs work games of high school players attending a nearby camp. Each one receives an evaluation of the game he or she officiates. Evenings find the students actively officiating; each ref participates in four games daily. At the conclusion of camp, each person receives an honest appraisal of her or his ability. The refs attend to expand their knowledge and skills with the hope that they can improve the level of games they work. Many do profit and move up; others may need further improvement that will come through experience. If you wish additional information, contact:

Nationwide Basketball Referee's Camp
4525 Jolyn Place
Atlanta, GA 30342

Other sports also offer similar schools, clinics, and summer camps. An example of a school for hockey officials is:

WHL School of Officiating
10333 Southport Road S.W., Suite 521
Calgary, AB, Canada T2W 3X6

Other camps, schools, and clinics include:

Rocky Mountain Football Officials Camp
2300 14th Avenue South
Great Falls, MT 59405-5023

Coast to Coast Referee School
P.O. Box 412
Ellenton, FL 34222 (held in Dallas)

MEAC Basketball Officials School
P.O. Box 20754
Greensboro, NC 27420

Professional Referee Observation School
3230 Durham Drive
Riverside, CA 92503

Opportunities exist in all areas for officials, but particularly in women's sports, certain minor sports, and with some college conferences. Salaries range widely; most officials earn approximately $50–75 per game for high school major varsity sports and from $100 to $300 (with major conferences paying more) at the college level. Professional salaries vary with the sport and the number of games.

The expansion of sports at all levels and the growth of women's participation guarantee opportunities for new officials. For energetic people willing to work hard and master all the rules of a given sport, this can be a promising part-time or even full-time career area.

Start Your Future Now

If officiating is potentially your career, pursue these suggestions:

1. Read about your future profession. Subscribe to *Referee*—it contains excellent information, updates, current happenings, profiles of successful officials, and suggestions for improving your skills.
   For a subscription, write:

   Referee
   P.O. Box 161
   Franksville, WI 53126

   Also read books on officiating, such as Richie Power's *Overtime* (Ballantine), Kathryn Davis' *The Art of Sports Officiating*

(Allyn and Bacon), John McDonough's *Don't Hit Him, He's Dead* (Celestial Arts), Edward Dolan's *Calling the Play: A Beginner's Guide to Amateur Sports Officiating* (Atheneum), and Eric Gregg and Marty Appel's *Working the Plate: the Eric Gregg Story* (William Morrow).

2. As suggested earlier, volunteer to officiate, wherever you can find an opportunity. Many exist. What you don't earn in salary you will in experience.

3. Study and master the rules for your sport. Stay aware of recent changes, interpretations, and emphases. The NCAA and high school athletic associations provide rule books.

4. Participate to the extent you are able in the sport of your interest.

5. Work to develop the personality traits of an official, such as independence, maturity, self-confidence, and a high moral character.

6. Study your sport and its officials. Use your imagination and make the calls. It will be good practice. Read technical books on officiating and on your sport.

7. Write to the administrative office of the league you might like to officiate and ask the requirements so you can begin to prepare. Each league (at all levels) will have a person performing the task of supervising and assigning officials. For example, for professional baseball, contact:

Office for Baseball Umpire Development
P.O. Box A
225 Fourth Street
St. Petersburg, FL 33731

CHAPTER FIVE

Sports Communicators

T he field of sports communication teems with opportunities. Jobs become available daily with newspapers, radio, and television because professional and college teams engage large numbers of people. In "sports show business," sports communicators rank near the top in the world in glamor, sheer fun and excitement, and oftentimes, financial rewards. Within the field numerous careers exist.

Sports Journalists and Sportswriters

Dramatic contrasts exist in newspaper careers. Paul Smith has written for a variety of newspapers including the *Harrisburg Patriot*, the *Wilmington-News Journal*, the *Philadelphia Journal*, the *Philadelphia Inquirer*, the *Pittsburgh Press*, and the *News-Dispatch* in Michigan City, Indiana. Smith has enjoyed assignments such as covering the Chicago Cubs and White Sox during the baseball season, Notre Dame football in the fall, and Indiana, Purdue, and Notre Dame during the basketball season, as well as local sporting events. His advice to aspiring writers: "The romantic bloom comes off the rose early in the profession, but if you stick with it, it has its rewards."

Contrast Smith's meandering with Tony Leodora, former sports editor at the *Times Herald* in Norristown, Pennsylvania, who served over 15 years with one newspaper. Following college Leodora took a position in business but was able to pursue his life-long interest in sports through working part-time at the newspaper as a stringer (correspondent) who would attend local events and write about them for the paper. Eventually Leodora decided to go full-time, and upon the retirement of the sports editor, he was promoted to that position.

Leodora's schedule varied. Mornings found him in the office; afternoons were free except when he had an interview or game to cover. Evenings found him covering an athletic event and then often returning to the office to write up his story and coordinate the sports pages; other times he was able to send his story to the paper via computer. He got excellent seats at all athletic events, met regularly with professional sports stars and coaches, occasionally traveled to events in other cities—and got paid for it all! In particular, he loved baseball spring training in Florida. But it was not all fun and games. There were many long days, and writing is hard (though enjoyable) work.

For many years, some of the finest journalism has been found on the sports pages of America's papers. It is here that lively, fast-paced, colorful action writing appears. Some sportswriters have become well-known for adopting a uniquely aggressive style, such as Christie "Jock Talk" Blatcheard of the Toronto *Financial Post,* Tim Murray of the *Los Angeles Times,* and Bill Conlon of the *Philadelphia Daily News.* The size, circulation, and location of the paper will determine to a large degree the activities of the sportswriters. The sports department of a small-town newspaper normally has an editor and one other writer, and perhaps a couple of part-timers who cover local weekend events. Such a paper will rely upon the wire services (such as Associated Press) for national stories.

A large-city daily may have a staff of 10; several of these will have a particular specialty, such as golf, football, boxing, or the high school scene. While these reporters cover other events during the off-season, they write several articles a week related to their expertise when their sport is underway.

Frequently, reporters work unusual hours and days. For example, those employed by a morning newspaper usually will work late afternoon and evening hours, five days a week, including Saturdays (if there's a Sunday edition). They then would have two weekdays off. Major papers will send a reporter along with the team to cover out-of-town stories. While this sounds glamorous, it frequently is time-consuming and hectic. Following the event, the writer will use his or her notes to prepare the article, looking for a particular angle or interesting aspect to highlight for reader appeal. The writer calls in the completed article (usually preparing and sending it via computer) and finally gets to sleep, usually about 2:00 A.M.!

Preparing for Your Sportswriting Career

Many opportunities exist on small, local, and weekly newspapers to begin your career. If a vacancy does not exist in sports, take a position writing news; it will help you build your craft of writing and will aid you in making a switch to sports when an opening occurs.

There are a lot of free tickets, but newspapers remain notorious for paying mediocre salaries to their professionals, and smaller papers pay even less. Of course, it's possible that you will gain a reputation and be given your own column, which could lead to a more substantial income. Having a column means that your work appears regularly in the same location in the paper, usually under your photograph. Your column would be commentary rather than straight reporting. In terms of your career, a column marks your success as a sportswriter.

At one time, reporters began their careers as copy aides, helping around the office by performing clerical tasks. Having proven themselves reliable, they might be asked to join the staff as cub reporters. This would involve small, unspectacular assignments eventually leading up to important tasks. Today, few sportswriters start this way. Most attend college and pursue course work in the department or school of journalism or communication arts. If you plan such a career, include several courses in writing; grammar skills will be a necessity. You also should consider building a strong background in the humanities and using your free electives in sports courses from the physical education program. Courses in photography will increase your chances of obtaining a job, particularly with smaller papers.

Sportswriter Jackie Lobin suggested for those still in school that while you're in your last two years of college, you make an especially strong effort to land a summer or part-time job on the local newspaper; constant new experiences are the key to becoming a good sportswriter. These experiences will greatly enhance your ability to obtain a full-time position following graduation.

Characteristics of Sportswriting

In recent years, the expansion of television and radio coverage of sporting events has resulted in a modification of newspaper coverage. A decline in straight factual reporting and an increase in features has occurred. Not only does the reader want to know what happened, but such additional information as the condition of the player injured, who might be traded, and the likelihood of the team's success against the next opponent. Some outstanding features have resulted from careful, excellent investigative research revealing serious abuses in sports. However, most common in features are interviews with an athlete answering a series of questions about an aspect of her or his career.

Despite its outward appearance, the life of a newspaper person has its lonely side. In fact, one observer found that "creative loneliness" is an important characteristic of successful writers. After the big game or press conference, the hard work of writing, editing, and rewriting must be completed alone—and prior to the deadline!

A newspaper writer has a very special obligation to society to remain vigilant for excesses that may destroy sports. Too frequently, athletes, coaches, and administrators have engaged for personal benefit in conduct detrimental to their own profession. Coaches have forced injured players to participate; athletic directors have condoned illegal recruiting; players have put their own importance above that of their team and their sport; youth league managers have played only to win; and coaches have publicly abused players for mistakes. Even some parents unduly pressure their children to be superstars. It is here that the writer can make an important contribution.

Career Opportunities for Sportswriters

The number of big-city papers has diminished in recent years; however, many papers have expanded and many others begun in new locations. Opportunities exist for well-prepared and knowledgeable candidates. In considering this career, sportswriter Jackie Lopin has said that sometimes it's glamorous, usually it's exciting, and *always* it's very hard work. Even the writers considered the best in the country will tell you that it took years and years of dedicated effort to develop their craft.

BOOKS.   Many writers also produce books as a sideline. This serves as a creative outlet for their talents as well as an additional source of income. A considerable market exists for sports books, and publishers often look for manuscripts from newspaper people. Sportswriters commonly will coauthor a book with a sports figure. Likewise, sports magazines seek freelance articles.

MAGAZINES.   The growth of national, regional, and specialty magazines provides a ready market for the sportswriter. While major periodicals (*Sports Illustrated, Inside Sports*) have full-time staffs, they often utilize freelancers for specialty pieces. *Sporting News* and similar national newspapers make extensive use of purchased articles. Although less lucrative, regional magazines buy manuscripts, as do a host of specialty publications—sports yearbooks, college and professional football and basketball game programs, professional and minor league game programs, college and professional media guides, and others. Specific sport magazines—*Volleyball, Muscle and Fitness, Soccer Magazine, Hockey Player, Golf Digest, Skiing Magazine, Swim Magazine, Tennis* and others—provide additional outlets. National publications of a general nature—*New York Times Magazine* and *Parade Magazine*, to name a few—often run sports stories. If you wish to write, and have the necessary skills, you should be able to find a format and an outlet.

Sportscasters

Soprtscasters have swept over the land of North America, settling down in every locale. They have fan support and strong ratings.

Most large cities in North America can boast of sports talk shows. Some even have all-sports radio stations with round-the-clock sports talk hosts, most of them excellent. In addition, nationally syndicated shows are offered by personalities such as Brent Musburger, Pete Rose, John Madden, and Pat Summerall.

The growth of sports talk radio has reached phenomenal proportions. Founded in the 1970s by sports talk giants Art Rusk, Jr. (WABC-AM), Don Henderson (WCAU-AM), Ira Faistel, and later Lisa Bowman (KABC-AM) and Pete Franklin (WWWE-AM), sports-based radio programs have become immensely popular. Not a substitution by a coach or a call by an umpire goes unchallenged by fans. Occasionally, the fans who phone in operate from a lack of knowledge about the essence or subtleties of the sport involved and, when challenged, become highly emotional and irrational, adding to the shows' interest. It is rumored some stations have banned certain callers!

Characteristics of Sportscasting

Trends marking the industry include a move away from the once-popular insult-screaming host toward the calmer, knowledgeable professional, and the use of the cohost. The latter trend opens the door for a rookie to join with an experienced partner, making for a successful show. The best talk broadcasts combine commentary by the broadcaster about the performance of local teams and players, interviews with interesting sports personalities, and specific telephone calls from listeners. A show with a theme, frequently utilizing editorial comments by the host as a springboard, seems to work best. This job requires excellent knowledge of many sports, as the broadcaster frequently is put on the spot, and it is only for people who love athletics. Broadcasters in their time off often attend games, practices, and press conferences. Some handle sports news for their station in addition to their shows.

Undoubtedly the best way to break in as a sports talk show host involves starting in a smaller market (yes, they have talk shows) or working first as a sports journalist—these shows frequently hire newspaper people part-time for weekends and for full-time positions.

Radio provides jobs in sports in addition to the talk show positions. Most major stations have a sports editor providing news and often commentary. And thousands of stations across the nation broadcast athletic events live. Professional, college, and high school games need announcers who understand the sport and can communicate the action clearly and colorfully. Normally, one individual provides play-by-play, while the other gives analysis. Successful radio broadcasting can result in a move to the big time, and big money—television!

Television announcers receive the best salaries and the greatest exposure to the public. They may be employed by a sports team or a TV station—or both. Some serve as the sports reporter on the station's news program. As such, they cover many areas, necessitating a good knowledge of at least the major sports. Although they may appear on the show only twice a day for four or five minutes, TV sportscasters spend most of the day preparing for their air time. Often this involves attending press conferences, interviewing players, and covering games. It's an exciting life that brings the sportscaster in close contact with the athletic world. Many try their hand at automobile racing, playing quarterback (in practice), and pitching batting practice as a promotion. These activities are arranged to increase viewer interest and to expand the announcer's credibility as someone knowledgeable about sports. In addition to very good speaking ability, writing skills are also essential, since most sportscasters compose the information they announce.

The growth of cable television, such as ESPN and a variety of local and regional stations, has expanded opportunities in television. Like network and local commercial stations, cable operators need game announcers, producers, program directors, hosts for interview shows and panel discussions, announcers to report game results, and interviewers for news stories, human interest pieces, and investigative reports.

Sports announcers have captured the attention of the public. Brent Musburger's career moves, John Madden's fear of flying, and Tim McCarver's honest criticism of players have made headlines.

In general, game announcers capture the most attention. As with radio, they fall into two categories: play-by-play or color specialists. The play-by-play announcer generally explains each play as it occurs and its relationship to the overall game. The color commentator, usually a former player, provides insights into certain techniques and strategies the coach or athlete may employ; he or she often will provide amusing anecdotes about players. Most recently there has been an attempt to carefully put together a team of announcers that will complement each other's abilities and contribute to the listener's enjoyment of the game. Many hours are spent by the staff in preparing for a game or event. Studying player's backgrounds, talking with coaching staffs, and meeting with public relations specialists help in this regard.

Sometimes a third person will contribute to announcing the game.

Beginning Your Sportscasting Career

Knowledge of sports and an excellent speaking voice are important prerequisites for a career in sportscasting; physical attractiveness looms important for the television positions. Donna de Varona, a TV sports communicator, cautioned that you should have both a sports and an academic background; it's very hard for someone who has never played or been on the line in a competitive sport to really understand the dynamics of the game. Therefore, it is useful to take many of the same courses suggested for newspaper and public relations careers, such as writing, public speaking, sports studies, and physical education. Similarly, try to become involved in sports at some level of activity.

If you do not wish to perform in front of the camera or a microphone, careers exist in the background. For example, technical personnel are needed to operate cameras. Producers plan show content, timing, and commercials. Positions as broadcast technicians also exist in radio and television. These individuals operate and maintain the electronic equipment responsible for transmitting the signals onto the airwaves.

If you did not attend college (or even if you did), consider attending a trade school designed for radio and television careers. These schools offer short, intensive courses and aid in job placement. If you wish additional information, contact the following organization with your request for a list of the schools in your area:

Career College Association
750 First Street N.E. Suite 900
Washington, DC 20002

For those interested in the world of sports broadcasting, consider attending a broadcasting school. A typical curriculum features classroom instruction, live practice, guest lectures, broadcasting, and critique sessions.

The Connecticut School Broadcasting offers courses in several states. For information, contact:

Connecticut School of Broadcasting
Radio Park
Farmington, CT 06032

Once you have obtained the necessary education, Keith Jackson of ABC-TV's "Wide World of Sports" has provided this suggestion: If you want to be a television sportscaster, begin where you are comfortable. You shouldn't be too eager to run for the big city when the smaller community affords the better learning experience.

Many, many opportunities exist at the thousands of radio and hundreds of television stations in North America. Here the novice can hone skills and learn the art of the professional. Some individuals so enjoy their jobs in small towns and cities that they stay and make it a career. Others will use this background as a springboard to the "big time."

For additional information on sports journalism, contact:

National Association of Broadcasters
1771 N Street, N.W.
Washington, DC 20036

National Association of Radio Talk Show Hosts
139 St. Botolph Street
Boston, MA 02115-4819

National Sportscasters and Sportswriters Association
P.O. Drawer 559
Salisbury, NC 28144

Sports Public Relations Specialists

The dramatic growth of sports public relations (PR) stems from two perspectives: first, the desire by the fans and the media to learn more—and more, and *more*—about their teams and their favorite players, and second, the desire by colleges and professional teams to develop and/or maintain a favorable opinion of their organization or institution. Public relations specialists work to obtain publicity to fill stadia, increase the visibility of colleges, and promote players. The activities vary with the size of the college. For professional teams, the PR program will vary with the team level; major league team agents will be busier than those at the lower levels. Another factor that will affect this office's work is the success of the team and its players. Playoff teams and those with superstars create great interest and consequently test the energies of the PR staff.

The work setting is usually superior for professional and major college sports public relations specialists. Offices feature comfortable arrangements with the latest equipment, and the seats at the games are prime!

At the major college level (Division I), the PR director is supported by assistants, a secretary, and a few interns (those studying for the profession). At the professional level, teams normally have a public relations staff consisting of a director, an assistant, a secretary, and a few interns. Smaller colleges will have a one-person office, a part-time person, or none at all.

One of the most enjoyable aspects of the job includes the opportunity to watch the game. Of course, pregame preparations are involved; for example, preparing news releases, compiling statistics, issuing credentials to the media covering the event, and arranging refreshments.

Some typical activities of sports publicists follow:

- *Prepare media guides*—Booklets containing information on players and teams, they contain statistics and records for the sport; in addition, at the professional level, team yearbooks are produced.

- *Arrange or conduct media briefings*—Meetings with newspaper writers and TV and radio reporters to bring them information about a player or team development.
- *Coordinate press conferences*—Meetings with the media for the coach and/or players.
- *Send news releases to media*—Usually two or three pages that provide new information and statistics for the newspapers, radio, and TV.
- *Send specific news releases*—These provide information to a player's hometown newspaper, for example.
- *Maintain files*—Collect information, including historical and statistical data, on athletes and teams.
- *Direct press box*—For certain sports, arrange for seating and materials for newspaper, radio, and television representatives, as well as for distribution of admission credentials.
- *Maintain scrapbook*—Clip newspaper items about the team(s) and players.
- *Provide and arrange for photography*—Arrangements for a photograph of each player (head-and-shoulders portrait called a *mug shot*) must be made, along with action team photos and video for TV. Videotape highlights and photographs are made available to the media.
- *Answer requests*—Give information to the league office, NCAA/NAIA office, other teams, and to the general public.
- *Write stories*—Not all newspapers send a reporter to cover an event, so a story often is written by the sports publicist and distributed to the press.

At the college level, the public relations specialist for athletics is called a sports information director (SID). If this position sounds demanding to you, you're right. Many days you work from 9 A.M. to midnight! When the team is on the road, a sports publicist goes, too. This may be a trip to the Rose Bowl in Pasadena or to the Rainbow Classic Basketball Tournament in Hawaii, but it more frequently means a six-hour bus ride to less glamorous cities or towns.

Discussing her role as senior vice president for communications for ESPN, PR pro Rosa Gatti said, "The primary objective of my department is to attain the most extensive and favorable exposure for the company in the media, in order to attract public interest in the network and, in particular, viewing of the network's telecasts."

Before joining ESPN, Gatti served as the first woman sports information director at a major college in the United States. She was named to this position at Villanova University and later held a similar position at Brown University. During this time, she held two executive positions: president of the ECAC (Eastern College Athletic Conference) and SID and vice president of CoSIDA, the College Sports Information Directors of America. She likewise paid her dues on many game days; she followed this rigorous schedule on Saturdays in the fall:

7:30 A.M.	Up and at 'em.
8:00 A.M.	Phone rings. Associated Press needs another press credential.
9:00 A.M.	Arrive at office; call football office for any recent developments, illness, injury, any changes, line-ups; put press passes in order and give to ticket personnel. Phone rings constantly: "Any tickets left?" and "Will the game still be played in the rain?"
10:00 A.M.	Visiting sports information director arrives; get opponents' statistics and press guides; he or she proofs roster in game program for mistakes; take care of additional press requests.
10:30 A.M.	Three student assistants arrive; transport materials to press box (game programs, mimeo machines, typewriters, food, and beverages).

10:45 A.M.	Stop to say hello to pregame gathering of alumni.
11:00 A.M.	Get to press box; check place cards for seating arrangements; see that phones for wire services are working, three sports information phones plugged in; check whether radio station's lines are live; go over pronunciations of players' names with visiting broadcasters (visiting SID does likewise).
11:30 A.M.	Press box crew and aides start arriving. These are: press box steward who checks passes; statisticians (three offensive, two defensive); play-by-play typist; spotters for the P.A. announcer; radio announcers; runners to hand out stats after each quarter; announcer; photographers (one for color, two for black-and-white on side line); coaches' game film photographers.
12:00 P.M.	Media start arriving; give injury update; emphasize special human-interest angle: "Our top receiver went to high school with their safety."
1:00 P.M.	Everyone set…countdown. Two students operate phone for calls from TV networks with updates on scores across country, and we give report on our game; student gives information to announcer on records being approached or broken; announce attendance, availability of coaches for interviews after game.
4:00 P.M.	Game ends. Get ready for second mad rush; run off stat sheets; students call in final score to television stations and other outlets; if not present, a student calls AP and UPI with 150 words on game.
4:30 P.M.	Write and do 60-second radio reports for local stations; give condolences to opponent SID about his or her team's loss.
5:00 P.M.	Start sending the reporters' stories (four to five pages each) via telecopiers (FAX)—it usually

	takes two hours by the time all reporters are finished wiring and each page is sent.
7:00 P.M.	Send statistics for both teams to NCAA computer center by telecopier for weekly compilation and release.
7:30 P.M.	Clean up and go home.

Planning Your Career as a Sports Publicist

People wishing to enter this profession must have appropriate course work in college with a major in journalism, public relations, communication arts, or a specialty in sports public relations within a sports management program. Publicists have greater opportunities to move up in the field than others in sports, as sports public relations departments expand and as individuals move up regularly. For example, Vic D'Ascenzo, former Sports Information Director at Fairfield University, first obtained a position as a graduate assistant coach in the basketball program at Fairfield. He had served as an administrative assistant for the basketball team at Villanova University as an undergraduate English major. He then received an appointment as assistant SID at Fairfield. Later he received his master's and accepted the position as director.

If you think you wish to gain employment at the college level, contact:

The College Sports Information Directors of America
Campus Box 114A
Texas A&M University
Kingsville, TX 78363

CHAPTER SIX

Sports Entrepreneurs

Nothing is more characteristic of the genius of the American people than is their genius for athletics. Nothing is more synonymous of our national success than is our success in athletics. If I were required to indicate today that element of American life which is most indicative of our nationality, my finger would unerringly point to our athletic escutcheon.

GENERAL DOUGLAS MACARTHUR
Past President, U.S. Olympic Committee

*I*f entrepreneurship is your thing, look no further than the numerous opportunities presenting themselves in sports and athletics. An examination of products and services available yields creativity in all sizes, shapes, and forms.

Elston Howard, former New York Yankees baseball star, developed the "donut," the round piece of metal placed on the bat when batters are loosening up in the on-deck circle prior to stepping up to the plate. Elmer Van Sickle's Medi-Exercise Ball provides exercise, development, and rehabilitation of injured players; the Strength Shoe (Strength Footwear, Metairie, Louisiana), a sneaker with a platform mounted on the bottom front, was developed to increase speed and quickness and improve vertical jump. Bill Raferty, broadcaster for ESPN, CBS, and Sports Channel, began Bill Raferty's Broadcasting School for those wishing to break into the electronic media. The litany goes on and on. Clearly, the entrepreneurial penchant of Americans, combined with their love of sports, yields an impressive array of business successes.

Perhaps this American spirit is best exemplified by NFL Films. In 1962, Ed Sabol took a number of risks. First, he submitted a $5,000 bid to the National Football League (NFL)—double the successful bid of the previous season—for the right to film the championship game. Second, he won the right and then filmed the game differently; previously, one camera stationed in the stands high above the fifty-yard line would capture the entire game. Sabol utilized several cameras around the stadium; one filmed entirely in slow motion. The result: "Pro Football's Longest Day." Former Commissioner Pete Rozelle's verdict: the greatest football film he had ever seen. Following a few years of adjustment, Sabol's company—NFL Films—emerged, transforming the way the world looked at professional football. Eventually the multimillion-dollar award-winning organization found itself on the cutting edge of film technology, business organization, and public relations—to the visual and audio delight of fans worldwide.

Product Development.   As with any business enterprise, product development often takes years. Mike Hall developed the "Determinator," a sophisticated pitching machine. Taking five years in development, Hall's device marries television and batting practice. A video of the pitcher (any pitcher) appears on the screen approximately 55 feet away, and at the appropriate moment, the ball is delivered through an opening. Hall believes his machine will revolutionize batting practice, as it closely approximates game conditions.

Hall came up with the idea for his invention following a dream. "I figure you get only one great idea in a lifetime," suggested the entrepreneur. As president of Video Baseball of America in Roswell, Georgia, he placed a machine in use at Fulton County Stadium for the Atlanta Braves. "The entire concept and idea is tremendous," stated Braves General Manager Bobby Cox.

Distribution.   Not all sports entrepreneurs develop and manufacture a product. Some focus upon distribution. The candy bars endorsed and named for professional players quickly come to mind. Perhaps a better example is Thera-Kinetics of Mt. Laurel, New Jersey. This organization assisted Tony Dorsett, Tim Kerr, John Elway, and other athletes and the general public with its CPM device. This machine provides continuous passive motion (CPM) to an injured or recently surgically repaired body part. Present thinking among orthopedic physicians in many cases calls for movement of the ailing limb as soon as possible following a medical procedure. Patients strapped to CPM move and exercise their limbs—recovery time is shortened. Jerold Zebrick, owner and president, has leased the high-tech equipment to hospitals, sports medicine rehabilitation centers, and individuals. The devices must be utilized under the supervision of a physician and the direction of a physical therapist or related health personnel. In commenting on the success of marketing his equipment to the sports world, Zebrick stated, "These guys are worth millions of dollars to their teams, and when they go down, the object is to get them back and playing as fast as possible." Fortunately for companies such as Thera-Kinetics, even most nonathletes want to return to normal activities as soon as possible following an injury.

Reading Materials.   The public's hunger for sports-related news has allowed a variety of newsletters, magazines, and other publications to flourish. Some examples are:

- regional and local publications covering sports news in a given geographical area
- newsletters and magazines supporting a single university's sports teams, or a professional sports franchise
- magazines and newsletters focusing on a single sport, such as wrestling or baseball

The ready availability of personal computers and desktop publishing software has made it possible for almost anyone to produce attractive, professional-looking publications. This means that if you choose to start a sports-related publication, you can get started on a small scale and then if conditions allow, grow into a larger enterprise.

The growth of the Internet is also opening up publishing opportunities related to sports. For example, Cloverleaf Golf Publications of White Salmon, Washington, produces a series of books on golf which can be down-loaded from the Internet by interested customers. Newsletters and other publications can also be produced and marketed on-line. If you want to start your own sports publication, this is one approach. An advantage is you can save on printing and mailing costs.

Lest it seem too easy, fun, lucrative, and glamorous to own your own sports-related company, as you mingle with and interview athletes and others from the sports world, heed the words of basketball yearbook guru Mike Moriarty: "It's not that easy to make money; the business side is difficult, and competition is hell. I spend most of my time on the nonglamorous end of the business." Moriarty started out by publishing the *Big East Yearkbook* on a part-time basis. The University of Missouri grad then expanded his enterprise and began publishing *The ACC Yearbook, The Big Ten Yearbook,* and *The Big Eight Yearbook.*

"Sports is something that appeals to everyone; friends are envious! However, if all I had to do is to watch games and edit stories, this [job] would be a blast. This is not an easy area to make money," Moriarty said.

The opportunities for entrepreneurship exist. Carefully choose a special niche, work like hell, and enjoy life as a sport entrepreneur. With any luck, financial success soon will follow.

Before starting a sports-related business, be sure to do your homework. Bookstores and libraries offer scores of books on starting and running your own business, and the local office of the

U.S. Small Business Administration is a great resource (see your phone directory for the nearest office).

For a brief overview, request the publications *Starting a New Business* and *Running a Small Business*. They're free on request from:

Consumer Information Center
Department 71
Pueblo, CO 81009

CHAPTER SEVEN

Sports Medicine Professionals

T hey do marvelous things combining the latest research, new technology, and a strong basic understanding of the human machine. They function as a team working to prevent injury, educate athletes, and restore players to normal functioning through rehabilitation. They are sports medicine professionals.

Among this team of specialists:

athletic trainer

chiropractor

dentist

exercise physiologist

nutritionist

strength, fitness, and conditioning coach

optometrist

orthopedist

orthotist

osteopath

podiatrist

physical therapist

psychologist

ophthalmologist

David Lamb, past president of the prestigious American College of Sports Medicine, defined the field: "Sports medicine is the scientific and medical aspects of exercise and athletics."

More specifically, Professor Henry Miller, M.D., of Wake Forest University in North Carolina divided sports medicine into three categories:

1. *Athletic medicine*—the evaluation, conditioning, and prevention and treatment of injuries.

2. *Research*—the physiological, biochemical, biomechanical, and behavioral aspects of athletic medicine. Includes finding new methods more successful and satisfactory than the present ones.

3. *Prevention and rehabilitation* of chronic and degenerative disease associated with sports and athletics.

A further clarification can be obtained from the American College of Sports Medicine, which is not a college in the traditional sense but a professional society composed of over 10,000 members. Its constitution states that the society is:

A multidisciplinary professional and scientific society dedicated to the generation and dissemination of knowledge concerning the motivation, responses, adaptation and health of persons engaging in exercise. Specifically, the college is concerned with:

1. Basic physiological, biochemical, biomedical, and behavioral mechanisms associated with exercise.

2. Improvement and maintenance of functional capacities for daily living.

3. Prevention and rehabilitation of chronic and degenerative diseases.

4. Evaluation and conditioning of athletes.

5. Prevention and treatment of injuries related to sports and exercise.

The organization, founded in 1954, has provided guidance and knowledge to sports medicine professionals and athletes in terms of the latest athletic health procedures based upon clinical practice and serious research. The college publishes position papers as well as research and information publications, sponsors research grants, certifies certain sports medicine personnel, and conducts workshops and conferences.

The explosion of sports injuries and serious concern about permanent damage resulted in the joint proclamation by the American Medical Association and the National Federation of State High School Athletic Associations of the Athlete's Bill of Rights. Sports medicine personnel, coaches, athletes, and others should carefully examine the list.

The Athlete's Bill of Rights

Proper conditioning helps to prevent injuries by hardening the body and increasing resistance to fatigue.

1. Are the prospective players given directions and activities for preseason conditioning?

2. Is there a minimum of two weeks of practice before the game or contest?

3. Is the player required to warm up thoroughly prior to the participation?

4. Are substitutions made without hesitation when players evidence disability?

Careful coaching leads to skillful performance, which lowers the incidence of injuries.

1. Is emphasis given to safety in teaching techniques and elements of play?

2. Are injuries carefully analyzed to determine causes and suggest preventative programs?

3. Are tactics discouraged that may increase the hazards and thus the incidence of injuries?

4. Are practice periods carefully planned and of a reasonable duration?

Good officiating promotes the enjoyment of the games as well as the protection of the players.

1. Are players as well as coaches thoroughly schooled in the rules of the games?

2. Are rules and regulations strictly enforced in practice periods as well as in games?

3. Are officials employed who are qualified both emotionally and technically for their responsibilities?

Right equipment and facilities serve a unique purpose in protection of players.

1. Is the best protective equipment provided for contact sports?

2. Is careful attention given to proper fitting and adjustment of equipment?

3. Is equipment properly maintained, and are worn and outmoded items discarded?

4. Are proper areas for play provided and carefully maintained?

Adequate medical care is necessary in the prevention and control of athletic injuries.

1. Is there a thorough preseason health history and medical examination taken?

2. Is a physician present at contests and readily available during practice sessions?

3. Does the physician make the decision as to whether an athlete should return to play following injury during games?

4. Is authority from a physician required before an athlete can return to practice after being out of play because of a disabling injury?

5. Is the care given to athletes by coach or trainer limited to first aid and medically prescribed services?

Obviously, adherence to these guidelines can serve to reduce the incidence of athletic injuries. Sports medicine personnel can make an important contribution through publicizing and orienting the athletic community to these suggestions.

Despite the apparently varied background of those involved in sports medicine, a common thread runs through their backgrounds: they have a greater interest and knowledge about science than most Americans; they have an academic orientation (most attend graduate or professional school following completion of college); they demonstrate a human-service orientation—a willingness to help people; they attempt to add new knowledge to their profession by sharing successful clinical practices and experimental research results; they enjoy people; and they like athletics and sports.

Considerable opportunities for variation exist in the sports medicine career cluster. People not wishing a lengthy college commitment might consider a position as a sports physical therapy assistant, while those more academically inclined might consider the life of the sports psychologist. Similarly, within the specialties, opportunities exist for several emphases. For example, an orthopedist would have these options: working at a sports medicine center while seeing patients and conducting research, or assisting a local high school as teams' physician and maintaining a private practice emphasizing sports medicine.

The following sections will explain the various sports medicine careers as well as providing information about general good athletic health procedures. Not only will people considering sports medicine careers find this chapter of value and interest—but coaches, athletes, and fans will also benefit.

Sports Physicians

Located at the core of the sports medicine team is the orthopedist. Orthopedists are medical doctors who perform the surgical miracles that return athletes to competition; in addition, they supervise the activities of allied health personnel. Orthopedists specialize in the health of individuals' bones and joints, related supportive structures, and muscles. Osteopathic (D.O.) and chiropractic (D.C.) specialists likewise can serve as sports physicians concentrating on their specific orientation to providing good health. Other medical specialists—for example, dentists—also may assist athletes. Regardless of the specialty of the physician, the commandments of Theodore Fox, M.D., formerly of the Chicago Bears professional football team, deserve serious attention as guidelines to behavior. These have undergone slight modification to conform to this book.

Team or Sports Physician's 10 Commandments

1. The physician must be trained in all procedures for prevention, recognition, diagnosis, and treatment of injuries; first aid; as well as knowledge of soft tissue and skeletal injuries.

2. The physician must personally examine and evaluate all candidates for the sport or team prior to their participation to determine each individual's fitness for the same. This should include a history of all previous illnesses, accidents, and surgical procedures as well as a psychological evaluation and a thorough physical examination. The physical evaluation should include observations of any injury, especially in the collision sports. The physical examination should include determination of the individuals' maturity, balance, coordination, agility, stamina, and strength.

3. The physician must know the fundamentals of the particular sport with which he or she is involved, to better understand the mechanism of the injuries occurring, as well as the injured participant and her or his problem.

4. The physician must observe and evaluate the emotional well-being of the athlete, especially the young player. Is the candidate being pushed by a frustrated parent to be a superstar or made apprehensive by a parent who is concerned that the athlete might get hurt?

5. The physician should select and *fit* all protective gear and equipment and check it as to type and quality, especially in the collision sports.

6. The physician should supervise the trainer or the coach in the proper use of physiotherapeutic techniques in the training room. Also, the physician is responsible for conditioning and rehabilitation exercises (such as weight training). Upon the doctor rests the responsibility for total rehabilitation of the injured athlete (mental and physical); a careful examination must precede the athlete's return to participation.

7. The physician must advise the coach not to teach dangerous blocking and checking practices and to avoid mismatches between athletes, especially young players. The doctor should

advise the coach or trainer about problems or injuries that may occur because of heat, humidity, overwork, or fatigue.

8. The physician (or a designated replacement) must be available at all times to examine the injured players as soon as possible after the injury. This is especially true in collision sports where, if possible, the physician should be on field. Often youngsters will mask an injury so as to continue to play; a physician can make an assessment of the severity of the injury. Also, certain injuries (neck, reinjury) require a doctor's examination.

9. The physician must prevent an injured player from returning to the game if there exists a reasonable doubt about his or her condition. In doing so, the physician must resist all pressures from coaches, parents, alumni, and the player.

10. The doctor must obtain X rays of injuries (and other information as necessary) prior to judging the condition of the injury.

The importance of the physician to sports may not be realized by the average fan, but the athlete recognizes the contribution. Gale Sayers, formerly an outstanding football running back at Kansas and with the Chicago Bears, gave his opinion in his fine book *I am Third* (Bantam):

> The business of injuries to professional football players is a tricky one, with all kinds of complications. You really have to leave it up to the team doctor. I have always found Dr. Fox a man I could rely on, a man I could go to if I had problems. My philosophy about aches and pains is to get them checked out to be sure they're not going to impair your performance.

Dave Meggyesy, also a former professional football player, echoed the significant role physicians play, recalling some negative experience in college (*Out of Their League;* Ramparts):

> When a player is injured, he is sent to the team physician, who is usually more concerned with getting the athlete back into action than anything else. This reversal of priorities leads to unbelievable abuses.

The sports medicine staff has a serious obligation to the player's present *and future* health. Close adherence to Dr. Fox's 10 Commandments will curtail many of the serious abuses related to athletics.

While a few teams, mainly at schools, employ general practitioners (GP's) in the capacity of sports physicians, orthopedists by their training best serve in this position. Those involved in sports normally serve on a consulting basis with teams and/or work in sports clinics.

This career is the best paid of all sports medicine personnel. Yearly salaries over $100,000 are common; most earn considerably more. In addition, sports physicians enjoy fine working conditions and, in most cases, great prestige.

Many sports physicians work under the auspices of a sports medicine clinic or center. These facilities work with individual athletes and with sports teams. Often they have contracts to provide their services to local schools and colleges. Some are actually associated with colleges, such as the Temple (Pennsylvania) University Center for Sports Medicine and Science; others are privately owned and operated, such as the Stone Clinic of San Francisco, California.

Typical functions of a sports clinic include:

- diagnosis and treatment of acute athletic injuries
- rehabilitation of athletic injuries
- referral resource for team and family physicians
- preventative education

A clinic or center's staff is made up of a team of sports medicine professionals: the orthopedists, athletic trainers, physical therapists, and other specialists on a consulting basis as needed, such as dentists or nutritionists. Most centers have the finest equipment, both diagnostic and rehabilitative. These centers frequently serve nonathletes who wish to avail themselves of the latest aggressive prevention, diagnostic, and rehabilitation procedures and, if required, surgery. The medical aspects of the center fall under the jurisdiction of the orthopedist.

Orthopedists attend undergraduate college and then enter medical school. After graduation, they concentrate on their chosen field. This involves more coursework, individual study, and practical experience. The internship takes one year and the residency normally four years, so the total education of the orthopedist takes nine years after college! During the residency period, the young doctor works under the supervision of an experienced orthopedic physician, conducting examinations, directing first aid, performing surgery, and designing rehabilitation programs. Not all orthopedists go into sports medicine; some set up private practice and work to correct deformities related mainly to muscle, joint, and bone problems. If a person has a serious accident requiring surgery, such as cartilage damage to a knee or hip replacement, an orthopedist would be involved. Some have very specific subspecialties and will focus upon surgical procedures relative to the ankle or knee joint. With increased attention to sports injury prevention and rehabilitation, opportunities for careers as a doctor with a speciality in orthopedics will continue to be very good.

Additional information concerning medical doctors (M.D.'s) may be obtained from the following:

American Medical Association
515 N. State Street
Chicago, IL 60610

Council on Medical Education
c/o American Medical Association

Association of American Medical Colleges
2450 N. Street, N.W.
Washington, DC 20037

American Orthopaedic Society for Sports Medicine
6300 N. River Road, Suite 200
Rosemont, IL 60018

Osteopathic Physicians (D.O.s), like medical doctors, utilize surgery, drugs, and other acceptable health care practices. In addition, they may use *manipulation* (treatment using the hands or mechanical means) and emphasize the treatment of the whole athlete in designing a conditioning or rehabilitation program. While still not totally accepted by medical doctors, osteopathic medicine has made great gains in recent years. In Detroit, all four professional sports teams utilize osteopaths as their team physicians. The educational requirements of osteopathic colleges almost parallel those of medical colleges, and osteopaths wishing to specialize likewise complete a rigorous residency. However, they are not certified medical doctors.

Salaries of osteopaths lag behind those of medical doctors. However, most do well—$50,000 to $100,000 a year or more—and those in sports medicine do even better. Opportunities for employment for osteopaths in the future will continue to remain very good as sports medicine expands and the public comes to further respect the work of doctors of osteopathic medicine.

As with medical doctors, osteopaths undertake residencies upon graduation from osteopathic college; for those interested in sports medicine, the residency will take from three to five years. Regardless of specialty, all D.O.s must obtain licensing in all states.

For those interested in sports medicine, osteopathy deserves serious consideration as a career choice. For additional information, contact:

American Association of Colleges of Osteopathic Medicine
6110 Executive Boulevard, No. 405
Rockville, MD 20852

American Osteopathic Association
142 E. Ontario Street
Chicago, IL 60611

Chiropractic physicians (D.C.s) emphasize the use of manipulation as their primary treatment. They believe that a person's (in this case the athlete's) health, to a large degree, relates to the welfare of the nervous system. Interference with the system thus impairs normal function and lowers resistance to disease. Chiropractors generally work with the spine to restore proper functioning to the nervous system. In addition to manipulation, they utilize water, light, massage, ultrasound, electric, and heat therapy. Often they prescribe a special diet, nutritional supplements, exercise, and rest to heal the injured athlete. They do not believe in using prescription drugs or surgery as part of their approach, nor are they permitted by the state in which they practice to do this, because they are not medical doctors.

More than 30,000 licensed chiropractors practice their profession in the United States. Most have private offices, while others work at clinics and chiropractic colleges where they engage in teaching and/or research. Those engaged in sports medicine usually make it known that they emphasize the treatment of athletes. Some teams maintain a chiropractor as a consultant, should they need such services.

A strong interest in sports medicine exists among chiropractors. In addition, some former athletes have entered the profession. For example, Dr. Fred Cox, former placekicker for the Minnesota Vikings professional football team, went on to become a D.C. The Council on Sports Injuries is an organization for chiropractors who are interested in the treatment of athletes.

The expansion and acceptance of chiropractic medicine will result in continued improvements in salaries, which currently lag behind those of physicians but may exceed $80,000 per year.

If this profession interests you, contact:

American Chiropractic Association
1701 Clarendon Boulevard
Arlington, VA 22209

Council on Sports Injuries
c/o American Chiropractic Association

International Chiropractors Association
1110 N. Glebe Road, Suite 1000
Arlington, VA 22201

Council on Chiropractic Education
7975 N. Hayden Road, No. A-210
Scottsdale, AZ 85258-3246

Athletic Trainers

Training athletes is the greatest profession in the world for helping people. The athlete trainer is a 24-hour father confessor to all, both men and women, young and old. I take great pride in being an athletic trainer and a part of the NATA.

Michael O'Shea MA, ATC, University of Louisville

Athletic trainers receive a specific education to serve in the sports world and are unique sports medicine personnel in that regard. Consequently, they often have considerable importance and influence over the direction of sports medicine at their institution and in general.

An athletic trainer's duties consist of the implementation of an injury prevention program and the initiation of immediate treatment and rehabilitation procedures for the injured athlete as directed by the team physician. He or she is the person you see down on the field or sitting on the bench close to the large first-aid kit. Long before the contest, the trainer has prepared the participants, taping some and providing therapy for others. He or she will stay after the game, providing services as needed.

Specifically, trainers engage in the following activities:

- Selecting proper equipment in cooperation with the coaching staff and the equipment manager. In this regard, new developments—such as those in pediatrics or dentistry—should be reported to the coaching staff.
- Supervising safety factors involving playing areas—that is, the removal of items players may run into and the repair of equipment constituting a safety hazard.
- Assisting in the application of injury-preventive devices, such as helping and assisting with braces and similar gear and reminding athletes to utilize such equipment if necessary.
- Planning a conditioning and injury-prevention program with the coaching staff and other sports medicine personnel.
- Maintaining the athletic training area and its equipment, including ordering supplies, supervising the servicing of equipment, and keeping careful health records.
- Administering first aid to injured athletes. This would involve both minor problems, like a sprained ankle, and major difficulties requiring transporting the player to a hospital.
- Developing and supervising a rehabilitation program under the supervision of a physician. This duty would include monitoring the use of exercises shown to the athlete, and it may involve the utilization of ultrasound or the whirlpool.
- Reporting to the coach and physician the rehabilitation progress of the athlete. This involves the gain of strength in the affected area as measured by technical equipment. This is one of the most important tasks of the trainer, as it involves determining how soon the injured player may return to action.
- Serving as an executive and educator. As an administrator, the trainer maintains a budget, develops a student trainers program, and supervises the student trainers. In a major athletic program, there is a head trainer, and he or she has a staff of assistant athletic trainers.
- Establishing and maintaining good interpersonal relationships with the coaching staff, the sports medicine consultants, and the players. The trainer serves as the head of the control center.

Telephone calls come in on the deposition of X rays taken of an injured athlete, coaches call to make requests about certain safety equipment newly available, and parents call to ask about an injury their child suffered; similar other requests regularly arrive. It's not a career for someone looking for an easy job.

If it seems that the athletic trainer has many tasks to perform, you are absolutely correct!

The importance of proper conditioning involving strength, cardiovascular fitness, and flexibility cannot be overemphasized. The following list contains the 10 Cardinal Principles of Athletic Conditioning that every coach, player, and sports medicine professional must know and implement. The specific accountability rests with the athletic trainer.

10 Cardinal Principles of Athletic Conditioning

1. *Warm-up*—Each activity must be preceded by an adequate warm-up. Stretching activities and running will provide the greatest benefit following a mild warm-up. Warming down (includes stretching again) likewise requires attention.

2. *Gradualness*—Start slowly to condition someone and look to peak at a certain time. Setting goals can be helpful.

3. *Timing*—Athletes must be counseled not to overdo workouts; relaxation and rest form part of every conditioning program.

4. *Intensity*—Workouts and practices must be characterized by quality and continuous activity with appropriate rest periods.

5. *Capacity level*—While cautious to avoid the above pitfalls, athletes will want to work to capacity and should have encouragement to do so.

6. *Strength*—Greater endurance, speed, flexibility, and confidence will result from improved strength.

7. *Motivation*—Sports medicine personnel can reinforce the coaches' techniques to stimulate players.

8. *Specialization*—Include exercises in each player's conditioning program to improve the player in relation to the sport he or she wishes to play and her or his weakness.

9. *Relaxation*—Trainers should familiarize themselves with specific techniques to teach players how to relax and thereby recover from tension, fatigue, and stress.

10. *Routine*—A planned daily, weekly, and monthly routine must be constructed for each player in cooperation with the athlete and coach.

Quite obviously, the duties and obligations are quite significant, and the athletic trainer's importance to sports continues to increase. Ortho Davis, trainer emeritus for the Philadelphia Eagles and executive director of the National Athletic Trainers Association, believed that the most important role of the trainer is to prevent an injury from occurring, because at the professional level a player cannot afford to miss practice. For the Eagles, conditioning occurs 11 months a year! After a month break following the season, many players begin a new program. Two days each week, running for cardiovascular endurance and agility is emphasized. Three days focus on weight training. Specific training to improve a weakness likewise occurs.

Many athletic trainers have management responsibilities. Serving in this role in a large university may involve supervising assistant trainers and other staff. It may also involve administering departmental budgets.

One of the most visible (via television) trainers is Ronnie Barnes. He serves as head athletic trainer for the New York Giants. Active in the National Association of Athletic Trainers, Barnes said, "If you're not good enough to play, yet still want to be in on the sports action down on the field or on the court, seriously consider the position of athletic trainer." Barnes served as athletic trainer at East Carolina University, where he received his bachelor's degree, and at Michigan State University, from which he obtained his master's degree before undertaking his present position. He also earned the Athletic Trainer Certificate (ATC).

Serving as an athletic trainer for the Giants may sound glamorous, and it is! "The profession demands hard work, long hours, and travel, but it's exciting," he said. "The profession is still in its infancy—I particularly enjoy the breakthroughs in terms of new ways to improve athletic performance, such as a new stretching program or weight-training regimen."

Despite the entry of large numbers into this profession during the 1980s, job prospects continue to look good. A number of high schools have added athletic trainers to their staffs. In 1985 North Carolina became the first state to require them for high schools, and this trend has spread. For example, Orange County, Florida, instituted a similar mandate in 1990. Andrew Clary, University of Miami head athletic trainer, noted that "the future in this job is tremendous, not only in school settings but in corporate fitness." Clary believes his profession makes a unique contribution to sports medicine because of its practitioners' unique knowledge of soft tissue (such as muscle). The undergraduate athletic training option at Penn State University typifies most programs. It includes the following courses:

Orientation to athletic training

Advanced athletic training

Recognition and physical examination of athletic injury

Foundation of therapeutic exercise

Exercise physiology

Introduction to therapeutic modalities

Administrative aspects of athletic training

Additional related courses and other university requirements round out the program.

While disappointed with the general level of salaries (an average of $34,000 annually in colleges, but $50,000 to $110,000 in the pros, according to the U.S. Department of Labor), Barnes stated, "Athletic training is still an up-and-coming profession. It is particularly wide open for minorities who have entered this career only in small numbers."

The major trainers organization, the National Athletic Trainers Association (NATA), certifies trainers, who receive the Athletic Trainer Certificate (ATC). NATA also evaluates college athletic training programs. Its address:

National Athletic Trainers Association (NATA)
2952 Stemmons Freeway, Suite 200
Dallas, TX 75247-6103

You may wish to examine the fine NATA publication *Journal of Athletic Training;* it contains a variety of articles by sports medicine personnel as well as professional information.

Similar services are also provided by:

American Athletic Trainers
  Association and Certification Board
660 W. Duarte Road
Arcadia, CA 91007

Another organization of interest is:

National Strength and Conditioning Association
530 Communication Circle, Suite 204
Colorado Springs, CO 80905

Sports Physical Therapist

Sports physical therapists work with athletes who have been disabled through accident, birth defect, or illness. Some therapists work with athletes sent to them by a physician to aid in the rehabilitation of an injury. Treatments include:

- exercises for increasing strength, endurance, coordination, and range of motion
- activities to facilitate motor capacity or learning
- instruction in activities of daily living and use of assistance devices
- application of physical agents such as heat and cold, sound, water, and acupuncture to relieve pain and/or alter physiological status

Physical therapists attend college to receive certification in their profession; some attend graduate programs and enter leadership positions in the field. Certification requires pursuing certain course work and, in 49 of 50 states, passing an examination to receive a license to treat patients.

A typical college program includes courses in the basics of physical therapy, physical agents, patient evaluation and treatment, therapeutic exercise and medical areas such as pharmacology and pathology.

Students also would pursue a regular complement of courses required by the college. In addition to their professional area courses and electives, they may wish to take work in sports studies and sciences, such as athletic training.

Many physical therapists who work with athletes do so at sports medicine clinics where they assist other professionals in rehabilitating athletes. This team approach undoubtedly will continue to characterize the profession for the future.

Salaries, typically in the $50,000 to $70,000 range, will continue to increase as the sports profession and the public come to realize the value of physical therapy.

If you wish additional information, read *Opportunities in Physical Therapy Careers* in VGM's Career Horizons book series, and contact:

American Physical Therapy Association
111 N. Fairfax Street
Alexandria, VA 22314

Other Sports Medicine Professional Opportunities

The fabulous growth of sports medicine has touched every area of the medical and allied medical professions. Specialists applying their unique skills and knowledge to improve athletic performance include dentists; vision specialists such as optometrists and ophthalmologists; exercise physiologists; psychologists; massage therapists; nutritionists; podiatrists; orthotists and prosthetists; and others.

Sports Dentists

When I've tried pitching without the mouthguard, I get tired quicker and feel more pain in my arm afterwards. Some might say it's psychological, but I don't think so.

HANK IERVOLINO
Former Baseball Pitcher
New York Technological University

One of the areas of sports medicine that has created excitement in recent decades has been the use of special mouthpieces. Interest in these devices skyrocketed following a 1980s *Sports Illustrated* report. Technically called a *mandibular orthopedic repositioning application* (MORA), this dental apparatus fits over the lower teeth and readjusts the misalignment from which some athletes suffer. The players reported increased overall performance and particularly improved strength. Dr. Richard Kaufman, a Long Island, New York, orthodontist and a pioneer in this field, noted, "It is essential to place the jaw in a proper position to enable the athlete to function at his maximum potential capacity. I have been conducting tests to show that injuries can be reduced and overall physical functioning can be increased by using a custom-fitted mouthpiece which places the jaw in optimum position."

While not all research agrees with Kaufman, there is general agreement that the position of the jaw has much to do with total body energy and muscle strength. Additional research is presently being conducted to validate the effectiveness of the MORA. Undoubtedly, for some individuals, this device will have a beneficial effect. For a dentist with an interest in sports, the ongoing development of special mouth devices makes this a very exciting career.

Most sports dentists serve athletes in many traditional ways. They work with players to help them avoid injury to the mouth area through the use of dental devices, if necessary, and other protection such as face guards in football and mouth guards in field hockey. The utilization of the mouthpiece and face guard has cut injuries by 60 percent. In addition, the dentists provide regular oral examinations; nothing will "bench" an athlete faster than an abscessed tooth. In the case of injury to the mouth, the dentist provides appropriate treatment.

Few, if any, dentists involve themselves with sports on a full-time basis. In addition to their regular practice, some dentists serve athletic teams as consultants. They are paid a yearly fee for their duties relating to the team. Others volunteer their services to school and community teams.

The American Dental Association (ADA) has outlined the general primary functions of the team dentist:

1. The dentist is responsible for making sure that players have good oral health at the start of the season.

2. The team dentist helps set up and implement the school mouth protector program. Each year, the dentist and school officials should discuss when the program should take place, how and by whom it will be run, what kind of protectors should be used, and what the cost will be.

3. The team dentist can treat emergency dental problems if the player's own dentist is not available, or can administer first aid if the team physician is not present.

The ADA provides additional suggestions, guidelines, and information to dentists to assist them in this highly specialized area.

The Committee on Dental Health in the United States Olympic Committee's Sports Medicine Council serves athletes and athletics in four ways. First, they serve in an educational fashion by helping athletes realize that total health includes "dental fitness." For example, a requirement was implemented that women participating in field hockey must wear a mouthpiece when playing under the auspices of the U.S. Olympic Committee. Committee members hope that this requirement will have an educational effect by trickling down to the college and high school level.

Second, the Committee on Dental Health screens athletes prior to international competition. In some cases, the treatment of an infected tooth has resulted in dramatic improvement in the athlete's performance. The committee not only works with athletes, but has also serviced fans at the Olympic Games.

Third, the committee provides remedial care and aids the athlete in securing dental care in or near the athlete's hometown. Consequently, the committee prepared a national list of dentists with an interest in and appropriate skills for working with athletes.

Fourth, the dental health committee fosters research, such as the experiments conducted on the value of the MORA.

Dental care should be part of the total training program of every athlete and every athletic team. Fortunately, coaches and players have realized this; in the future, many opportunities will exist for the dentist interested in sports medicine.

The education of a dentist is a long, arduous process. It requires excellent academic performance in high school, college, and professional dental school. However, the rewards are great. Sports dentistry can provide the opportunity to work with athletes on an ongoing basis and, for those interested, the chance to invent and develop dental devices contributing to increased athletic performance.

Additional information about dentistry can be found in the book *Opportunities in Dental Care* (VGM Career Horizons Series) and from:

American Dental Association
211 E. Chicago Avenue
Chicago, IL 60611

Sports Vision Specialists

> It used to be that athletes would go to the eye doctor, read the chart, and either be given a prescription for glasses or be sent home. That was then. Today there are options.
>
> THE ATHLETIC EYE
> (Seiderman and Schneider)

Historically, most individuals and athletes have been measured for their static visual acuity (SVA)—how well they could read a stationary eye chart while seated. However, athletes don't function in their sport in this fashion. Enter *dynamic visual acuity* (DVA)—how well moving players see moving objects. Today's sports vision specialists emphasize the importance of visual acuity to athletic success and techniques to enhance such skills, particularly DVA.

Bausch and Lomb's Council on Sports Vision has discovered these early warning signs for detection of vision problems:

• athletes who squint to see clearly

- football players who have difficulty seeing the ball and catching passes
- tennis players who have difficulty focusing on the ball and reacting to the serve
- golfers who have trouble discerning the distance to the green
- basketball players who are uncertain in their ball handling, miss too many free throws, or tend to close one eye when they shoot
- athletes who constantly rub their eyes or suffer from headaches or excessive tearing.

While most of the public, including athletes, remain unaware of the dynamic value of vision, Steven DeVore and Greggory DeVore have had excellent results working with a variety of athletes. Results of the DeVore brothers' technique, have included:

- At California State University at Hayward, two of the lowest-ranking tennis players tried the technique. The results made international news. Their coach commented, "In all my years of coaching, I have never seen such rapid progress in athletes before."
- Doug True, who played on the University of California basketball team, utilized the system to improve his shooting percentage. He later was drafted by the Phoenix Suns of the National Basketball Association.

This training system has the potential to attract more and more athletes, and additional sports optometrists (and optometric assistants and technicians) may be necessary to implement this program or others of its type.

For people thinking of a career in a sports-related profession, one of the most exciting and rewarding will be in sports vision. Dr. Burt Fisher, who has assisted members of the Dallas Cowboys and other teams, lamented, "It seems odd that parents and coaches will spend so much time developing a young athlete and so much money purchasing the necessary equipment and padding and then ignore proper eye care." Fortunately, the message of Dr. Fisher and his fellow sports vision specialists has begun to attract attention; future players in all sports at all levels will give serious attention to this aspect of human performance.

As with other medical personnel, the education and training of ophthalmologists (M.D.'s) and optometrists (D.O.'s) requires a serious commitment and long study. One important criterion for success is an interest in science and academics. Opportunities also exist for paraprofessionals to serve in this area as technicians and assistants. Normally these will require shorter training, in a trade school or community college. Salaries are considerably below that of eye doctors.

For additional information, consult the book *Opportunities in Optometry* (VGM Career Horizons Series) or contact the professional organization of optometrists at the following address:

American Optometric Association
243 N. Lindbergh Boulevard
St. Louis, MO 63141

Exercise Physiologists

Breakthroughs in physical training and fitness conditioning occur continuously. Despite a string of broken records and superior athletic successes, additional information needs to be discovered. Heading the movement to maximize athletic performance are exercise physiologists. Those involved in athletics normally work at sports centers, some located on college campuses, and perform the following major functions:

- assisting serious and weekend athletes to achieve fitness
- developing team conditioning and injury prevention programs with coaches and other sports medicine personnel
- evaluating the potential of athletes
- helping players to recover from injury
- working with world-class athletes to improve their performances.

The underlying assumption of exercise physiologists (who most often work closely with a variety of other sports medicine professionals) is that through analysis of the elements of athletic prowess, they will be able to teach athletes to perform even better. Consequently, across the nation and the world, new research continues to provide innovative methods of evaluating performance and training techniques.

One area of major contributions has come in the realm of women's athletics. Just a couple of decades ago, sports and athletics generally were believed to be too demanding and too intense for most women. Fortunately, the myth that women cannot engage in conditioning and training activities has largely disappeared. Professor George Colfer of Texas A & M University reviewed the research on women and physical activity and developed the following conclusions:

1. Women can be athletically skilled and rigorously trained.

2. Women are perfectly capable of performing strenuous activities without any physical impairment.

3. Active women possess a better state of health than those who are inactive.

4. Women are capable of high-level motor tasks as well as those involving endurance capabilities.

5. Strength can be developed or improved in women at a higher ratio than that of men.

Colfer concluded that the training needs of women are basically the same as those for men, and there is no reason to invent different training techniques for women.

Typical of the people entering the exercise physiology profession is Jill White. An athlete in basketball and track at Brittenkill High School (New York), she completed her undergraduate degree at Ithaca College, then enrolled in the exercise physiology program at the University of Delaware where she earned a master's degree. She then pursued additional graduate studies at the University of Georgia.

"I was always very interested in athletics (my father is a college coach) and science, and when I found out you could study sports science, I was ecstatic," said White.

Exercise physiologists utilize modern technology to complete their tasks. Slow-motion films, videotapes, and computers give clues for perfecting performance. For example, by using a biomechanical computer analyzing the placement of the joints of the body, scientists have discovered that keeping the feet flat against the ground throughout the entire throwing motion will yield the greatest distance for the javelin thrower.

In analyzing performance, Dr. Marvin Clein, founder and director of the University of Denver Human Performance Laboratory, explained some of his procedures: "The first thing you look at when you test an athlete is the ability to use oxygen." Clein stated that the physical capacity to deliver powerful explosive force (arm power or leg power) serves as an important prerequisite. The laboratory looks at other aspects of the athlete's physiology. For example, bowed legs can assist football running backs; fast-twitch muscle fibers react well to quick-moving, high-intensity sports; narrow hips enable long-distance runners to amass medals.

Following the receipt of her doctorate at the University of Miami, Pat Mosher put her knowledge of exercise physiology to good use. She joined the faculty at the University of Tennessee at Chattanooga as director of the school's Human Performance Laboratory.

"This is a great career for people-oriented persons who enjoy helping their fellow human beings, and it never gets tedious," noted Dr. Mosher. "I love what I'm doing and I'm very enthusiastic about seeing people improve." She had the experience of working and conducting research at the University of Miami's Human Performance Laboratory while earning her master's and doctorate. Dr. Mosher recommended that in addition to a strong background in science, course work in physical education and computers will prove beneficial.

The career of exercise physiology remains wide open for employment for people interested in the sports aspects of the work of exercise physiologists. The preparation requires the completion of a master's degree (M.S.); many students also complete the doctorate (Ph.D.). Frequently, exercise physiologists with master's degrees will gain employment in corporate fitness centers or sports medicine centers.

Many universities with an interest in sports medicine prepare exercise physiologists through interdisciplinary course work with a strong science emphasis. For additional program information, write to the colleges of your choice; address your letter to: Director, Exercise Physiology Program.

Sports Psychologists

The game of sport has changed—now the athlete must be in great shape not only physically, but also mentally. For some, this involves the use of sports psychologists.

One of the fastest-growing and most interesting of careers is that of sports psychologist. These individuals utilize the methods and techniques of psychology and related fields to maximize performance and well-being. Essentially, they aid the athlete to gain a competitive edge over rivals.

Typical are the cases from the files of Henry R. Reiter, a New York sports psychologist with success in working with a variety of athletes in tennis, golf, boxing, swimming, and professional baseball.

One of his clients was a 14-year-old, semisuccessful, female tennis player. Although intelligent, she unfortunately had a terrible temper and following a mistake would throw a tantrum. Her great potential was not being realized—frequently she came close but never won a major tournament. A program was set up to work with her and her parents over a six-month period. It included some hypnosis and self-hypnosis, relaxation therapy, and the rule that the parents did not attend tournaments. The therapy was designed to help lower the player's tension level and help her gain better control over her emotions. One technique dictated that following a mistake, she would silently count—3, 2, 1—and then yell, "Next point!" She began to win and went on to become a successful collegiate tennis player at a California college.

A professional golfer on the pro tour had difficulty with concentration. At this point in his career, he was earning enough to cover his expenses. However, with some training on concentration, he became a more successful golfer, in both skill and income. Dr. Reiter explained that "this was an easy case; sports psychologists have had excellent results assisting in improving athletes' concentration."

A professional baseball pitcher became a client of Dr. Reiter, who noted, "He had no self-confidence—I mean zero—and he was slightly paranoid." During a period of five months, meeting twice a week, the use of hypnotherapy and hypnosis helped the pitcher develop confidence. He asked to be traded to begin anew in a different environment. He was traded, and he has become very successful.

Most sports psychologists entering the profession today have a master's, and usually a doctoral, degree. In the past, people with backgrounds in athletic training, exercise physiology, and physical education might have functioned as sports counselors. However, the advent of malpractice lawsuits has quickly changed this situation. Those lacking appropriate degree work in psychology and counseling will be unable to obtain necessary malpractice insurance.

The doctoral degree requires both intelligence and persistence. When in a college program, take additional courses in the social or behavioral sciences with a major in psychology, and take sports studies or physical education courses when possible. While some universities have specific doctoral programs in sports psychology, most students wishing to enter this profession attend doctoral programs in clinical psychology. Within such programs, they apply the psychological concepts and theories to sports and athletics and, most importantly, undertake their training in clinic work with sports clients, utilizing psychological applications in their work. The latter is done under supervision. The doctoral dissertation work focuses upon sports psychology. Several master's level programs exist for students not wishing to pursue doctoral studies.

Sports psychologists operate in a number of settings—as consultants to teams, as college professors, and as private practitioners maintaining an office practice. It is not unusual to find many serving on a college faculty and on a part-time basis working with teams or individuals. Salaries for these individuals range from $50,000 to $100,000 or more—the pace often runs hectic, but most enjoy the combination of academic (college) and practical (working with clients).

Team psychologists most often gain employment with a professional team on a contract basis. They work on specific goals with the team, collectively and individually, and are available if needed in a time of crisis. They may handle such individual problems as substance addiction or loss of confidence as well as team difficulties including surviving a losing streak and coping with an irrationality, like an opponent with a "jinx" over them.

It's an enjoyable life style that also can be financially rewarding. Dr. Reiter commented that "one of the joys of this job is to see one of my clients reach their potential and enjoy doing it. Another reason I like my job is I really enjoy the variety of people with whom I work."

Bob Rotella of the University of Virginia succinctly summarized the dominant feelings toward his field: "Many athletes and coaches find a fuller understanding of the role of the mind and emotions most helpful in enhancing performance."

This appreciation of the value of this young field has come because many athletes benefit from the profession's methods. Julie K. Anthony formerly served on the staff of the Philadelphia

Flyers hockey team. She taught relaxation exercises to some of the players: "The player sits in a relaxed position and progressively tenses and relaxes all the major muscles in the body." The players practice this twice a day for 15 minutes; eventually they get to the point where, with a few deep breaths, they can tense and relax to finally relax the entire body. Anthony explained its value: "In the game, if the score is close and he is waiting to go in, an athlete can use this technique to prevent getting too tight."

Another technique of the profession—hypnosis—has aided several athletes. Bill Buckner, a former first baseman who was a fine hitter with several major league baseball clubs, hit a serious batting slump at one point during his career. Buckner stated, "When things are going wrong, sometimes its hard to analyze it. Under hypnosis, I was better able to talk about my batting motion and what I was doing wrong. Then, when I was still hypnotized, Dr. Misel reminded me of the things I should be working on." Buckner experienced excellent success following his counseling.

Most recently, the technique of "imagery or fantasy" has received a lot of attention. Recent research has shown that once athletes advance beyond the beginner stage, mental rehearsal, combined with the physical practice as opposed to practice alone, is more effective in preparing for an event. Steve Hebb, as a member of the U.S. Alpine Ski Team, used to sit and mentally visualize himself making his run: "I see myself making a perfect turn in the toughest part of the course." Dr. Richard M. Swinn of Colorado State University said that "this technique can be beneficial in ridding the athlete of negative [thinking patterns]."

Sports psychology is booming as amateur and professional athletes begin to realize its value and begin to take advantage of these modern techniques. In addition, weekend athletes wanting to improve their golf game or jump shot are availing themselves of these strategies. While few full-time positions have developed, opportunities seem promising. The success in conditioning the mind of athletes promises continued growth of the sports psychology profession.

For additional information contact:

The Academy for Psychology of Sports—International
6161 Busch Boulevard, No. 126
Columbus, OH 43229

The Journal of Applied Psychology
P.O. Box 1897
Lawrence, KS 66044

North American Society for the Psychology of Sport and
    Physical Activity (NASPSPA)
Department of Exercise and Sport Science
University of North Carolina at Greensboro
Greensboro, NC 27412-5001

Sports Massage Therapist

Professional, amateur, and weekend athletes, in their continuing
desire to prepare their minds and bodies for the test of competition, have discovered sports massage therapy.

Howard "Dr. Bucky" Grace of West Town, Penn., observed that
"those athletes who avail themselves of massage seem to derive a
greater benefit than their less athletic counterparts." Grace focuses
his energies and his "magic" hands on the entire body, then gives
special attention to the part of the body relative to the athlete's
sport. For example, runners would get extra treatment for their legs;
many athletes indicate to the therapist areas of extra emphasis.

Neal Sherman, an Illinois massage therapist, commented, "I
combine a judicious combination of Swedish massage and rolfing.
A lot depends upon the athlete's personality, game (type of sport
specialty), and the injury history of the athlete." Some athletes
prefer the laying on of the hands prior to an event or practice to
prepare for the competition, while others prefer a massage after-
ward to facilitate recovery.

Some teams employ massage practitioners to work with their players to promote circulation, alleviate stress, and aid overall well-being. The University of Florida's women's tennis and gymnastics teams and the National Hockey League's New Jersey Devils have utilized such services.

The education requirements for massage practitioners vary according to individual states. Many states do not require certification. However, there exists a growing movement from all massage specialists to have taken training from appropriate schools, and those institutions have proper accreditation.

Interested persons should check with the following organizations to locate a program:

American Massage Therapy Association
820 Davis Street, Suite 100
Evanston, IL 60201-4444

Associated Bodywork and Massage Professionals
28677 Buffalo Park Road
Evergreen, CO 80439-7347

Sports Nutritionists

For centuries, people engaged in athletics looked for "the edge"—something that would enable them to produce an excellent, competitive performance. This pursuit usually centered on conditioning and stamina, and more recently on weight training, stretching, and mental toughness.

The rapid major advances in nutrition and the growing awareness of them by the public, the medical establishment, and the sports establishment will catapult sports nutritionists into a major role in the years ahead.

Most nutritionists involved in sports serve in a consultation capacity with coaches, teams, and individual athletes. They offer suggestions regarding weight control, pregame meals, and vitamin/mineral supplementation. They usually are associated with a sports medicine center, a clinic, or a college.

Professional sports nutritionists may have backgrounds and education in either medicine or nutrition. Some also may have obtained their training as dieticians, nurses, athletic trainers, and physical therapists. Through additional study and reading, the latter individuals have prepared themselves to serve the sports community as nutritionists. For example, Jim Corea, a physical therapist, undertook additional college studies in nutrition in graduate school. He used the background in developing a Philadelphia radio program as well as in his daily practice.

One individual in this field, Dr. Sarah Short, a professor of nutrition at Syracuse University, developed an interest in computerized sports nutrition. Dr. Short has investigated the nutrition requirements of various athletes (football players, wrestlers, swimmers, and others) in terms of protein, calories, minerals, vitamins, and other nutrients. The increase of such attention to sports nutrition may encourage allied health personnel to gravitate to the field of nutrition.

Michael Colgan, director of the Colgan Institute in Encinitas, California, has studied the impact of nutrition on athletes, provides nutritional information, and writes regularly on fitness and nutrition. The Colgan Institute has received contracts to investigate the value of diet and mineral, vitamin, or herbal supplementation on conditioning, strength, and performance of athletes.

Another nutritionist, Dr. Ann Grandsean, founded the International Center for Sports Nutrition in Omaha, Nebraska. "The center encourages scientific research and provides information to athletes and physically active people interested in the benefits of good nutrition," Dr. Grandsean explained. She has also served as the chief nutritional consultant to the United States Olympic Committee and to the University of Nebraska athletic department; in addition, she has worked with the Chicago White Sox. Dr. Grandsean said "there is a genuine need to rapidly translate the most current research findings into easy-to-understand, useful, and factual information for athletes, coaches, and others involved in the training of our amateur athletes."

Some medical schools offer a medical degree (M.D.) with a specialty in nutrition, and many additional graduate schools provide a doctorate (Ph.D.). For those not wishing advanced study, some schools of allied health science offer a bachelor's degree (B.S.) in nutrition.

Some individuals enter this field with a degree in physical education, dietary science, chiropractic science, or nursing. This may provide an initial background, but considerable additional study must be undertaken to understand the complex biochemical needs of the body. Some individuals with training in naturopathic or holistic medicine do well in this field.

For additional information contact:

American Dietetic Association
216 W. Jackson Boulevard, Suite 800
Chicago, IL 60606

The International Center for Sports Nutrition
502 S. 44th Street, Suite 3012
Omaha, NE 68131

Sports Podiatrists

It's a rare sport that does not put great strain on the participant's feet. For the estimated 80 percent of all people who have foot problems, even minor ones, the increase of physical activity can worsen these situations.

These difficulties normally lead the injured party to the office of a podiatrist. These health professionals, usually identified by the initials D.P.M. (Doctor of Podiatric Medicine), specialize in foot care. Utilizing medical, surgical, and physical techniques, they work to prevent or treat foot injuries and diseases.

Dr. Lee Cohen of Morton, Pennsylvania, developed a Cush-ioned Anti-Pronation Insert (CAPI) for athletes. The device serves as a shock absorber and is part of Dr. Cohen's preventative approach to sports medicine. He stated, "It's no fun to see 40 or 50 people a day complaining of pain. It's more efficient to take some preventative steps ahead of time." Dr. Cohen further said that "we need to make the change from sports medicine to sports-injury prevention."

Additional information about this profession may be obtained from:

American Academy of Podiatric Sports Medicine
1729 Glastonberry Road
Potomac, MD 20854

Sports Orthotists and Prosthetists

Following several elbow problems with players, the New York Islanders hockey team contacted Andy Myers, a specialist in orthotics and prosthetics. He designed a brace to control the extension of the elbow; the affected players used it regularly in practice and occasionally in games. Their elbow problem was controlled significantly.

What are orthotics and prosthetics? These two related sci-ences, while frequently linked together, involve separate special-ties. Orthotics involves the use of bracing to correct and support a body part, while prosthetics concerns the utilization of artificial replacement limbs. Orthotists would be more likely to become involved with athletes. However, because a growing number of handicapped people are successfully participating in sports, it would not be unusual for a prosthetic specialist to design a limb to enable an athlete to participate, for example, in gymnastics or football.

Although certified in both areas, Myers has concentrated his efforts in orthotics. Within this field, his subspecialties include pediatrics, sports medicine, and spinal deformities. For example, one device he has constructed to assist athletes is the body jacket (known in the profession as an *anterior flexiform spinal orthosis*). Myers has used the jacket to treat football linemen and gymnasts for a fracture of the vertebrae of the spine. This injury is common to those types of athletes because of the stress and impact they put on their back and spine. The body jacket has enabled these people to return to practice and competition.

Myers is typical of people who have recently entered the field. He graduated from the program of prosthetics and orthotics of New York University. Following placement in the field, working under the supervision of a certified professional for one year each in prosthetics and orthotics, he took his examinations to become certified. Satisfactory completion of these comprehensive tests qualifies a person as certified, and the designation "C.P.O." may be placed after the name, such as "Andrew M. Myers, B.S., C.P.O." Now the individual can engage in the profession.

If this field appeals to you, you may wish to contact the following organization for additional information:

The American Orthotic and Prosthetic Association
1650 King Street, Suite 500
Alexandria, VA 22314

Sports Medicine Paraprofessionals

Love sports but don't wish to experience extensive education? Consider a career as a paraprofessional.

Numerous paraprofessionals assist in a variety of capacities in the sports medicine profession. The term *paraprofessional* here refers to health personnel who assist professionals (doctors and physical therapists, for example) in the performance of their duties. These aides, with advanced training and under supervision, recently have been permitted to undertake many of the duties previously handled only by professionals.

Specific characteristics of paraprofessionals include:

1. *Paraprofessionals serve under the supervision of a professional.* The amount of responsibility given to the paraprofessional varies with experience and training. For example, a physical therapy assistant may provide rehabilitation instructions to an injured high school basketball player with a sprained ankle.

2. *The career usually requires the completion of an education/training program, normally at a college.* Some paraprofessionals may have shorter programs. For example, most podiatric assistants receive on-the-job training. However, to become certified, they must pass an examination prepared by the American Society of Podiatric Medical Assistants. On the other hand, physical therapy assistants are required in most states to complete a two-year college training program, followed by a state exam for licensing.

3. *The nature of the paraprofessional's education/training resembles that of the profession to which it corresponds, except that it is shorter and more limited in content.* For example, the physical therapy assistant program typically includes curriculum courses such as anatomy, physiology, psychology, physical therapy procedures, and philosophy of rehabilitation. However, it is not as detailed or lengthy as the course work required for certification as a physical therapist.

Paraprofessionals now work in many sports medicine fields. This offers the individual with an interest in sports medicine the opportunity for an enjoyable and rewarding career. Following are some examples of these occupations.

Medical Assistants and General Sports Medicine Aides

It is possible to attend college for two years and obtain a degree as a medical assistant. The program at Arkansas Tech University focuses upon general knowledge combined with science courses and those related to office procedures and medicine.

Somewhat related are medical secretarial curricula. A number of business schools and community colleges around the country offer programs combining word processing or secretarial courses with courses on medical topics.

Many sports medicine professionals and clinics employ individuals as aides. These people, most of whom learn their duties on the job, assist both professionals and paraprofessionals. Many become very interested in their career and will seek schooling to improve themselves and their salaries. If you are interested in the occupation, apply directly to the private offices of sports medicine professionals or to centers that specialize in sports medicine. Often these jobs provide excellent insight into the world of sports and make good summer positions. In addition, future job opportunities will continue to expand.

Sports Podiatric Assistants

Podiatric assistants help podiatrists perform functions related to the medical health of the sport participant's feet. Among the assistant's duties are recording patient histories, preparing instruments and equipment, applying surgical dressing, preparing patients for treatment, assisting with routine office procedures, and similar tests.

While many programs are developing to educate podiatric assistants, most receive on-the-job training. Many qualify for the designation PAC (Podiatric Assistant Certified) from the American Society of Podiatric Medical Assistants. Eligibility for certification requires membership in the society and the passing of an exam prepared by it. Normally, certification carries with it improved prestige and increased salary. For additional information, contact:

American Society of Podiatric Medical Assistants
2124 S. Austin Boulevard
Cicero, IL 60650

Physical Therapy Assistant and Aide

Two paraprofessionals aid the physical rehabilitation patient—the physical therapist assistant and the physical therapy aide. Assistants graduate from a two-year program with a major in physical therapy, while aides typically learn on the job. Both of these types of paraprofessionals work under the supervision of a professional physical therapist, who in turn works under the supervision of a physician. For more information, contact:

American Physical Therapy Association
1111 N. Fairfax Street
Alexandria, VA 22314

Other Sports Paraprofessionals

A variety of additional sports paraprofessional careers are available to interested sports medicine enthusiasts. The following organizations can provide appropriate information:

Sports Ophthalmic Assistant & Technician
Joint Commission on Allied Health Personnel in Ophthalmology
2025 Woodlane Drive
St. Paul, MN 55125-2995

Sports Optometric Assistant & Technician
The American Optometric Association
243 N. Lindbergh Boulevard
St. Louis, MO 63141

Orthotist-Prosthetic Assistant & Technician
The American Board for Certification
   in Orthotics and Prosthetics
1650 King Street, Suite 500
Alexandria, VA 22314

Dental Hygienist
American Dental Hygienists Association
444 N. Michigan Avenue
Chicago, IL 60611

Dental Assistant
American Dental Assistants Association
203 N. LaSalle Street, Suite 1320
Chicago, IL 60601-1225

National Association of Dental Assistants
900 S. Washington Street
Falls Church, VA 22046

Certifying Board of the ADAA
203 N. LaSalle Street, Suite 1320
Chicago, IL 60601-1225

Dental Technician
American Dental Association
211 E. Chicago Avenue
Chicago, IL 60611

National Association of Dental Laboratories
555 E. Braddock Road
Alexandria, VA 22314

You may also wish to consult the book *Opportunities in Paramedical Careers* in the VGM Career Horizons series.

CHAPTER EIGHT

Physical Educators

G ym teachers, more properly called physical education
(PE) specialists, have long occupied an important place
in the hearts of youngsters. A background in PE can lead
not only to jobs as physical education teachers, but also to many
sports and health employment opportunities. Coaches often
come from the ranks of physical education teachers—so this, too,
looms as one of the attractions of the profession.

Many states have regulations similar to the following: each student in each grade shall participate in a planned program of physical education. The planned program shall include activities
which:

- encourage each student to attain and maintain a desirable
  level of physical fitness
- develop competencies for life-time participation in sports,
  team sports, and games
- promote an understanding between regular physical activity
  and health
- provide sports, games, and other physical activities that promote self-confidence and the ability to work in a group
- require coeducation instruction at the elementary, middle
  grade, and/or junior high school levels.

Current Trends
in Physical Education

In recent years, there has developed an increasing desire to educate young people regarding the importance of fitness, the joy of sports and athletics, and the value of lifetime sports. The President's Council of Physical Fitness and Sports defines physical fitness as the "ability to last, to bear up, to withstand stress, and to persevere under difficult circumstances where an unfit person would be ineffective or would quit."

Part of this concern for youth fitness has stemmed from cross-cultural comparative studies in which American youth fall below their international counterparts. In addition, the desire to improve the nation's health has focused attention on the school PE classes. For example, one study found "39 percent of the boys and 33 percent of the girls aged 11 to 18 overweight." Further studies show that "an overweight twelve-year-old has only a 20 percent chance of being a normal-weight adult. By age 18, that chance drops to 5 percent!"

Much as school curriculum changes in recent decades have occurred in other school subjects ("new" mathematics, "new" social studies), there has developed a "new fitness." It has taken several forms. Some of the most interesting have been the Play Factory at Emporia State University in Kansas and the New Games popular on the West Coast, which have emphasized the fun aspects of sports. Such programs have been based on concerns that people should have fun and that more people should participate in fitness activities, as opposed to focusing on winning or losing. This all represents a kind of throw back to traditional play, community play, children's games, social recreation—to the time when people played together as a way to grow closer. Some people who are not generally athletic or who have been inactive for years have been drawn to the new orientation. Physical education teachers have organized such activities at their schools with success. The leisure revolution has resulted in a desire to expand participation in lifetime sports. These new directions will continue to challenge and tax the energies and talents of physical education specialists.

In the last two decades there has occurred a strong movement toward skill development in PE classes. Meshed with the new fitness, this can prove extremely beneficial in aiding young people. Gone are the days when PE instructors would throw out some balls and sit and watch the kids play or play only softball because that's the sport the teacher enjoyed best.

Quite obviously, many demands and duties characterize the activities of the physical education specialist. The following is a sampling:

- determines the ability of students in their courses
- revises instruction based upon students' abilities, that is, in teaching a skill (throwing a ball), making it relative to what the class is able to do, and proceeding from that point
- prepares an equipment and materials purchase budget and maintains it once obtained
- utilizes an efficient system for reporting accidents and following them up
- conducts special programs for children with physiological and psychological problems
- provides information to the parents and community concerning the curriculum
- promotes physical fitness in the school and community
- helps students to commit themselves to self-improvement
- prompts nonparticipating learners to join class activities and stay involved
- develops a wide variety of skills in students, such as accuracy, agility, balance, coordination, flexibility, power, rhythm, strength, timing, and other psychomotor abilities.

A Typical Day

The physical education instructor must maintain fitness, not only as a model for students, but also to keep the rigorous schedule that makes many demands upon the teacher. Consider a typical day in the life of a community/junior college PE instructor who serves as a basketball coach. Frances Garmon, who has served at schools including Delta State College in Mississippi and Temple Junior College in Texas, has summarized a typical home-game day at the latter:

5:30 A.M.	Alarm clock rings—arise.
6:20 A.M.	Depart for college.
6:33 A.M.	Stop at store for three area newspapers; check the accuracy of game time and location.
6:45 A.M.	Arrive at gym and office.
6:50 A.M.	Check dressing room to see if everything is in order for the game—warm-ups, uniforms, shoes, socks, and training supplies.
7:00 A.M.	Call all local radio stations to remind them once again about the game. Make a short tape over the phone for radio broadcast. Leave any game-related information for the athletic office secretary.
7:45 A.M.	Review for class.
8:00–8:45 A.M.	Teach tennis class.
8:45 A.M.	Talk with and help students after class.
9:15 A.M.	Check to make sure the following people are prepared for the game: officials, clock operator, 30-second clock operator, ticket takers, scorekeeper, announcer, concessions workers, and business office personnel. Also call to make arrangements to have game videotaped.

10:00 A.M.	Call the national office (NJCAA) and give them choices for top 20 rankings. Check mail. Call opponent to check if everything is okay and obtain arrival time of team.
11:00–11:50 A.M.	Teach swimming class.
12:00–1:00 P.M.	Lunch.
1:00–3:00 P.M.	Office work.
3:00–3:30 P.M.	Check out sound system, videotaping equipment, 30-second and game clock, and all support personnel; have athletic secretary and cheerleaders call news media.
3:30–4:30 P.M.	Go home: change and shower for game.
4:35 P.M.	Return to gym.
4:40 P.M.	Doublecheck dressing rooms, gym lights. Go over game strategy.
5:30 P.M.	Meet with Temple team, discuss game plan.
6:00 P.M.	Greet visiting team; manager shows them to locker room. Talk with coach to see if everything is okay; may need location of a restaurant for postgame meal.
6:30 P.M.	Taping and individual talks with Temple team. Stretching exercises in locker room.
7:00 P.M.	Team takes floor for warm-ups. Coaches report starting lineups.
7:15 P.M.	Return to dressing room.
7:25 P.M.	Return to court; player introductions.
7:30 P.M.	Game begins.
9:00 P.M.	Game concludes. Talk with team in the dressing room and then with the news media.
9:30 P.M.	Check on dressing rooms; have managers and cheerleaders call news media not present at the game.
9:35 P.M.	Prepare statistics.
10:30 P.M.	Stop on way home for a snack.

| 11:15 p.m. | Prepare for following day's classes; prepare practice schedules. |
| 1:00 a.m. | Bedtime. |

For those individuals who mesh teaching and coaching, it's truly an unbelievable commitment. This combination requires intelligence, great energy, and solid ability, but it promises great rewards.

If you wonder why they do it, Pennsylvania teacher and coach Janet Lippincott offered an answer. She said, "When these students begin to play on a school team, I know they already have a good background in technical vocabulary and body mechanics and can concentrate on perfecting skills and various strategies." By teaching students at both levels, she can see carryover of their learning, reassess the class curriculum depending on their needs, and, best of all, watch their growth and development.

Education

Physical educators must obtain state certification as teachers. This takes place at a college that has an approved program for the education of teachers. In West Virginia University's program, for example, students take courses in four different areas: foundations, professional physical education teaching, activities, and a second teaching field and professional education. In addition to required courses, students may also take a variety of electives in areas such as coaching, an academic area, or dance. Students examine a wide variety of practical and interesting topics in courses such as:

Early childhood activities

Movement education and rhythms

Teaching wrestling

Teaching volleyball

Teaching dance in physical education

Curriculum in physical education

Principles and problems of coaching

Techniques of coaching

Water safety instructorships

The excellent program at the University of Wisconsin at La Crosse exemplifies basic course requirements. Some of these follow:

Physiology of exercise

Human motor behavior

Biomechanics

Orientation to exercise and sports science

Safety, first aid, and CPR

Adventure theory for physical educators

Human anatomy and physiology

Management and instruction in physical education

Evaluation in health and physical education

Teaching health-related fitness

In all programs for certification, in addition to professional physical education subjects, courses must be undertaken in the arts; biological sciences; history and social sciences; and mathematics. Program requirements such as these attempt to provide the student with a well-rounded cultural education appropriate for a college graduate.

Student teaching is a special experience that is part of the certification program. This activity finds the college students, under the supervision of a cooperating teacher and college faculty member, instructing elementary, junior high, or high school students. It is a period of intensive training. In other fields, it would be called an internship, residency, or practicum.

Most physical educators pursue graduate courses and a master's degree; a few will earn doctorates. Some will obtain graduate degrees in physical education, while others will undertake work in other areas. Florida State University offers special courses of study leading to a Master of Science or Doctor of Philosophy degree in motor learning and exercise physiology. The master's program has two areas of emphasis: (1) exercise physiology and (2) behavior with a track in motor learning/control. The doctoral program has subspecialties in anatomy, biomechanics, and exercise physiology. Florida State offers other programs in physical education at the master's and doctoral level, specifically designed for teachers and those wishing to enter administrative positions. PE teachers obtain master's degrees for professional growth, financial reasons, and often to satisfy a state requirement. For a faculty position at a community college, an advanced degree is a necessity. For those wishing to obtain a position as a PE department chairperson, advanced graduate work is required. Those seeking employment at the four-year college level will need to obtain a doctorate.

Job opportunities have greatly improved for PE teachers in the 1990s; in addition, salaries presently are good and will continue to improve.

Getting Started

If physical education instruction may become your career, visit with a PE teacher and discuss your plans. He or she will be able to suggest a college as well as provide hints. In college, build into your program courses in communication arts, science, and business to permit greater flexibility upon graduation. While teaching may be your first choice, career opportunities expand daily in sports and athletics. It is strongly suggested that you obtain a student membership in your professional curriculum organization to help you stay current with your career and with potential job opportunities. Write to:

American Alliance for Physical Education,
    Health Recreation, and Dance
1900 Association Drive
Reston, VA 22091

CHAPTER NINE

Other Careers for Sports Nuts

This chapter briefly covers a variety of other careers related to sports and athletics. The people whose jobs will be examined include equipment managers; statisticians; sports academicians; sports photographers; sports cartoonists; sports agents and representatives; sports museum workers; sports facilities architects, engineers, and drafting specialists; sports careers and the Internet; and sports organizations for women. Finally, this book offers an inside look at the world of professional wrestling.

Equipment Managers

Sports equipment managers oversee the handling and care of everything from baseball bats to football helmets, largely at the college and professional levels. The equipment manager has the responsibility of keeping the team's equipment clean and in good repair, having the equipment available for practice and games (this means traveling with the team), and providing security for the equipment, which is the greatest problem of the equipment manager. Often the manager is aided at the professional level by an assistant and at the college level by the teams' student managers. Most equipment managers also perform other tasks needed by the team.

People employed in this profession normally have a great interest in the sport with which they are associated; often they have played or coached, and some have worked as salespersons of sports equipment. While no special training or education is necessary, a knowledge of the equipment and the ability to perform minor repairs is important. Also, the personal qualities of reliability and punctuality are a must.

Although equipment managers have been actively performing the craft for over 100 years, their professional organization has existed for only a few years. Presently salaries are attractive. Most equipment managers earn salaries from $18,000 to $50,000 annually, with the higher salaries coming at the professional level.

Bob Lambert has served as equipment manager at Villanova University and also at the professional level. These jobs have kept him close to sports and allowed him to travel. "The job opportunities are great, and it's a wide-open area for women," Lambert said.

For further information, contact:

Athletic Equipment Managers Association
6224 Hester Road
P.O. Box 790
Oxford, OH 45056

Statisticians

Sports trivia buffs and rotisserie league fanatics can no longer claim exclusivity over sports statistics. Coaches have expanded their interest in this area, and the computer has emerged as a potent weapon in the arsenal. The data supplied by the computer add to the coach's knowledge of her or his team or the opponent; this information can assist with decision making. For example, the computer can process a great deal of data and find patterns. Football scouts can provide the computer with statistics on an opposing team, and then program it to provide information such as what play the team tends to run in a given situation. For example, the computer might predict that when losing in the fourth quarter, the opposing team tends to pass to the tight end on third down.

Statistics are kept at most levels of play. Which information is kept depends for the most part upon the philosophy of the coach. In basketball, one coach may want only rebounding statistics on the players; another may keep shot charts (locations of shots taken) and records of turnovers (the number, and who committed them); and still others may keep vast amounts of other information on their team and opponents. This may include such detailed information in a scouting report as the number of passes made between each player during a basketball game. Many high school and some college coaches record extra statistics, those over and above the minimal information kept by the official scorer.

High school and college coaches can be greatly aided by a competent student or volunteer statistician; likewise, the individual can gain valuable experience. Normally the coach will have a prepared form on which to record the information. The coach will explain the procedures to be followed and will allow the aspiring statistician to gain some experience in intrasquad and preseason scrimmages. Once the season begins, the coach will expect perfect accuracy. Interested individuals may wish to approach a local coach about aiding a team with statistics.

Experience will prove helpful. If you lack the background, you may wish to practice taking "stats" when watching a game or event. While this is quite minimal, it might convince a coach of your desire to serve as a statistician. A knowledge of personal computers, data entry, and programming also will prove to be beneficial.

Careers as a sports statistician remain quite limited on a full-time basis; however, several opportunities do exist to follow this job as an avocation. It should be mentioned that developing some skill in this area will help in related areas, such as sports information and newspaper careers.

Perhaps someday you will emerge as the Sultan of Stat as director of the Elias Sport Bureau—the keeper of records for the National Football League, the National Baseball Association, and a consultant to ABC's Monday Night Football, *Sports Illustrated*, and many other organizations.

Sports Academicians

In addition to the professional programs offered by schools and departments on college campuses (physical education, sports medicine, sports administration, and other), academic departments often offer sports-related courses.

Several scholars have begun to examine various aspects of sports from the perspective of their academic areas of study. These individuals have approached athletics and organized sports in systematic ways, armed with an excellent knowledge of how to conduct in-depth studies of a particular topic.

SPORTS HISTORIANS examine such topics as the biographies of famous athletes and trends from past decades, such as the origin of a sport. They also work to encourage high school teachers to incorporate athletics into their courses when teaching U.S. history. Frequently, these individuals publish articles in the *Journal of Sports History* for the appreciation of the reader and the expansion of knowledge.

SOCIOLOGISTS sometimes study the role of sports in society. For example, they investigate topics such as racial problems, attitudes toward winning and losing, the effect money has had upon athletes, socialization through school sports, and social stratification among athletes. Often they publish their findings in the *Sociology of Sport Journal*, the *International Review of Sport Sociology*, and other scholarly periodicals.

Like other academics, most sociologists teach in colleges. Those with special interest in athletics frequently offer courses with titles such as "Sociology of sport" or "Sport in American society."

ACADEMIC SPORT PSYCHOLOGISTS examine such subjects as running therapy, mental toughness, and the psychology of coaching. These individuals have a particular interest in the mental aspects of athletics. Frequently, they provide guidance to players and coaches concerning how to achieve greater success through closer attention to the psychological aspects of athletics. They work with coaches on topics such as motivation and the establishment of smooth working relationships with players; for the players, it means areas such as mental aspects of relaxation and of pregame preparation. Their articles appear in psychological and professional coaching journals.

PHILOSOPHERS with an eye toward sports have involved themselves in teaching courses and writing for the *Journal for the Philosophy of Sport*. They often deal with ethical issues.

Most jobs for sports academicians exist at the university level. This means that if you have an interest in this career, you will need to attend college at the undergraduate level and then continue through graduate school until you obtain a doctorate. A love of reading and scholarly activity is important as well as an ongoing desire to add to the body of knowledge of sports. Interested? Perhaps someday you may teach a course entitled "The contribution of athletics to American culture" or "Management techniques for sports facilities," or conduct and publish research on "The mental aspects of pregame preparation" or "The value of sports in a small town."

Sports Photographers

Want to be close to the action on the field or the court but have no penchant for coaching, officiating, or sports medicine? Then consider photographing or videotaping the event. Sports photographers capture on film some of the beauty of sports. A good sports photographer possesses excellent skills developed through many years of experience. If this sounds too demanding, consider beginning your career by "shooting" an amateur competition with a small camera or a rented video camera. If your interest grows, purchase equipment. Many local newspapers need photographs; ask them if they would like some of yours. You may even be paid! At the very least, you should receive a name credit with the photo. Many teams would greatly appreciate a video of their game for players and coaches to study. This may be an opportunity to gain some experience while aiding the team.

Jerry Gay, a successful, award-winning sports photographer, traced his love of his profession to his youth. In junior high school, he dreamed of someday becoming a big football star, but his dentist advised him to avoid all contact with sports while he was wearing braces. So he became a photographer. He has said that becoming a successful photographer is like becoming a successful athlete in that it takes a lot of hard work and patience to make the major leagues—but when you get there, you're glad you paid your dues.

Some photographers work for specific magazines or newspapers. If these are general publications, the photography staff will cover subjects other than sports; while a few photographers may specialize in athletics, they well may be called upon to work on other assignments. Naturally, those employed by sports magazines or newspapers would work only in athletics.

A significant number of photographers in this field work as freelancers. This means they are self-employed and contract to work for a number of publications. Some will receive specific assignments to cover particular events and will sell the shots they take. Others will work part-time for a couple of newspapers, supplying them with several photographs a week. Still others may attend games and hope they will get some photos of a spectacular event to sell to a magazine or newspaper.

Mike DiTrolio of Havertown, Penn., used his experience as a videographer to produce sports-related video tapes. He has produced football highlight films for Auburn, Maryland, and Rutgers universities as well as for professional teams such as the Philadelphia Flyers. He has also made recruiting videos for many college sports teams. DiTrolio said, "The nicest thing about shooting sporting events is that it's exciting! I want to be ready to capture the great play—the touchdown in the end zone.

"There exists a significant difference between running my own business and working for someone else," DiTrolio pointed out. He previously worked for TelRa, a video firm headquartered in Wayne, Penn. "My business and interpersonal skills, in addition to my videos, need to be excellent."

Few opportunities exist for sports photographers; however, a small group do very well financially, combining excellent salaries with a glamorous life. You may wish to consider it simply an avocation (hobby) or an enjoyable second job. If you think you're interested, start now, and take a photography, film, or video course in an evening school.

For additional information, consider reading the book *Opportunities in Photography* in the VGM Career Horizons series and writing to:

Photographic Society of America
3000 United Founders Boulevard, Suite 103
Oklahoma City, OK 73112

Sports Cartoonists

He has captivated the sports fans of New York, who have avidly turned for years to the pages of the *New York Daily News* to follow his exploits. He is—sports cartoonist extraordinaire—Bill Gallo.

Bill Gallo captures in hand-drawn art the activities of New York players, teams, coaches, and owners—to the delight of his followers. In addition, he often also deals with national issues. Although Gallo has entertained the greater New York area for decades, few other papers or magazines have added a cartoonist's work to enrich the sports pages. Consequently few full-time positions exist for this specialized craft. Evan Gallo writes on boxing as a columnist as part of his job at the *News*.

However, being a part-time sports cartoonist can serve as a profitable and lucrative hobby, and some magazines and papers have moved in this direction. For example, Vic Harville has provided sketches for the *Arkansas Democrat* with his "Sportstuff" cartoons, and Stephen Mellus has sketched "Draft Choices" for the *Middletown Record* in New York. A slow growth should occur in this career, with most sports cartoonists obtaining part-time positions.

Sports Agents and Representatives

In this era of fantastic salaries for professional athletes, the agent has become a visible member of the sports scene. "Show me the money" has become a catchphrase related to this profession. Agents, sometimes called representatives, act as the players' intermediaries with the team's owner and general manager in order to secure the best financial and playing arrangement for the athlete. The use of agents occurs in several professions; for example, writers use literary agents, and people in show business use booking agents.

Agents are usually lawyers or accountants. They obtain their salary as a percentage of the income the client will receive from the team (or athletic event, as in boxing). Agents normally receive 3 to 15 percent for their negotiation of the contract. When you consider the salaries of individuals like Ken Griffey, Jr., Steve Young, Penny Hardaway, John Elway, and Michael Jordan, you realize that this sports career can provide excellent salaries.

Shelley Pennefather, former college All-American and basketball star for the Nippon Express team in Japan, said a good agent is critical to a player's success. "My agent, Bruce Levy, was particularly helpful in my continuing basketball following college," stated Pennefather.

In addition to negotiating contracts, many representatives serve as financial agents for players, making suggestions for investments or product endorsements and handling income taxes. Some act as representatives for organizations, such as the football players' association, or for baseball's umpires. In doing so, they work to obtain better salaries, retirement benefits, and improved working conditions.

Sports Management Companies

Today, the trend is away from the single agent and toward the sports management company. For example, Pro Ex (Professional Excellence in Sports, Inc.) in San Diego, Calif., provides a full range of services for the professional athlete.

"The Pro Ex team of consultants allows us to offer the professional athlete an unmatched wealth of information to ensure the success of his career, both on and off the field," stated founder David Morway. Services range from contract negotiations and estate planning to product endorsements and public speaking development.

ProServ, based in the Washington, D.C., area with additional offices around the world, has athletes under contract in a wide variety of sports. One of the nation's premier sports management firms, it has had excellent success in obtaining endorsements for its numerous clients, including Boomer Esiason, Michael Jordan,

Greg LeMond, Brandy Johnson, Karch Kiraly, and Stefan Edberg. In addition, ProServ has organized events for companies to sponsor in the field of sports and athletics. In the fast lane of sports excitement and sports show business, only individuals with high energy levels and excellent negotiating and interpersonal skills should seek employment with a sports management company.

Many of the one-person firms have evolved into management companies for their individual clients. They may manage clients' moves and arrange product endorsements, earning a percentage of the profits in the process.

Agents for Nonathletes

Another important trend has been the movement for nonathletes associated with sports to seek agent representation. Presently professional and college athletic coaches, radio sports talk show hosts, television game analysts, umpires, and other sports-related people utilize agents to handle their contractual arrangements.

Typical of agents representing these individuals has been Richie Phillips. As a well-known attorney and representative for several players and coaches as well as the Major League Baseball Umpires Association and National Basketball Association Officials, Phillips has played an important role in negotiating contracts. Phillips said that "the representative lends objectivity to a situation, since the player or management may not be able to evaluate the athlete's contribution to the team, that is, the player's bargaining position." He has served his clients through careful examination of the language of contracts; for example, the wording of no-cut clauses. "If you're interested in the career, attend law school and do a good job for your clients," suggested Phillips.

For many years, players made their own arrangements with the team owners. With the introduction of television, rivalries between leagues, and the expansion of players' legal rights, salaries accelerated greatly. Many athletes in past years were underpaid for their performance; today some players are grossly overpaid. Hopefully, a leveling of salaries will occur before sports are seriously damaged in terms of public support.

Opportunities for agents in the future will remain small (presently there are approximately 2,500 agents in the United States and Canada), but the salaries will continue to be excellent. If you're interested, the best background is law and accounting meshed with outstanding communication skills, because if you can't convince an athlete to become your client, you can't get to first base!

The following book may prove beneficial to aspiring agents: *An Athlete's Guide to Agents* by Robert Ruxin, published by Stephen Greene Press.

Sports Museum Workers

Want to work in a sports museum?

Sports museums and halls of fame in North America stretch from Winnipeg (Aquatic Hall of Fame and Museum) and Toronto (Canada's Sports Hall of Fame) to Fort Lauderdale (International Swimming Hall of Fame) and Daphne, Alaska. (The American Sport Art Museum and Archives). They stretch from coast to coast, encompassing Cooperstown, N.Y. (National Baseball Hall of Fame and Museum), and Springfield, Massachusetts (Naismith Memorial Basketball Hall of Fame) in the East through Canton, Ohio (Professional Football Hall of Fame) and Stillwater, Oklahoma (National Wrestling Hall of Fame) in the Heartland to Vancouver (British Columbia Sports Hall of Fame and Museum) and San Diego (San Diego Hall of Champions) in the West. And they all (close to a hundred facilities) need employees!

Typical is the College Football Hall of Fame in Kings Island, Ohio. The facility houses several exhibitions, serves as a resource center for inquiries on the sport, and contains a library.

Most museums have film/video showings and other interesting activities. Most museum personnel fall into two categories: the business group and the professional/creative staff. The business people manage the financial aspects of the facility (budgeting, fund-raising, promotion, and advertising), while members of the creative staff design shows, assist visitors, direct library and reference services, and generally make the museum a fun and educational place for guests. The museum or hall of fame exists to honor a sport and translate the joy of it to others. The number of employees varies with the popularity and size of the museum.

For those interested in business positions, a regular college business program with a major in marketing or management would prove beneficial. Those with course work and/or special skills in fund-raising, public relations, and managing public (non-profit) organizations will have an edge in garnering jobs.

Programs also exist for those on the museum's technical side. For example, Baylon University, the University of Southern California, and other schools offer programs in museum studies. Write to any college in which you are interested and ask about museum studies options.

The following organization may also prove helpful:

International Association of Sports Museums and Halls of Fame
101 W. Sutton Place
Wilmington, DE 19810-4115

Sports Facilities Architects, Engineers, and Drafting Specialists

- The Skydome in Toronto
- Pilot Field in Buffalo
- The Camden Yards Twin-Stadium Complex in Baltimore
- The Florida Suncoast Dome in St. Petersburg

• New Comiskey Park in Chicago

These sports facilities are but a small sample of the recent sports projects constructed in North America. These structures, and numerous others on college campuses, provide wonderful opportunities for employment for people with special training in engineering, architecture, and drafting. Growing fan attendance, the desire to upgrade older facilities, and continued expansion of professional franchises have resulted in a surge of new facilities and restructuring of existing ones. Individuals who combine a love of sports with specialized skills and knowledge will have the opportunity to personally have an impact on the game(s) they admire. Architects, engineers, and often public relations specialists work on the initial design with the facility's owner. Speaking and interpersonal skills remain critical for these positions because often political leaders, voters, and others need explanations of the structure—and oftentimes of related costs and construction delays. Drafting specialists work as part of the design team under the supervision of architects and engineers.

A leading organization in the area of sports facilities design is Hellmuth, Obata and Kassabaum (HOK). Located in Kansas City, this organization and its team of sports architects and related personnel (drafters, secretaries, and others) study "the feasibility, design, and development of sports and spectator facilities." The group's successes include Bradley Center Area (Milwaukee), Memphis Downs Race Track (Memphis), Joe Robbie Stadium (Dade County, Florida.), The Alamo Dome (San Antonio), University of Delaware Sports and Convocation Center (Newark, Delaware), New Comiskey Park (Chicago), and Pilot Field (Buffalo).

If this exciting field interests you, consider attending college and studying architecture or engineering. These careers require a demanding academic program. A quicker, but less lucrative, route might be studying drafting at a trade or technical school or community college. All of these individuals must not only have a great knowledge of their profession, but also an in-depth knowledge and love of sports. For example, Ron Labinski of the HOK Sports Facilities Design Team on a visit to the Kansas City Chiefs' Arrowhead Stadium, where he served as project architect, noticed that the ceiling tiles had been removed above the taping tables. Upon further investigation, he found that the tiles had been taken out because many football players liked to *stand* on the athletic training tables for the taping of their ankles. Consequently, when involved with the development of Giants Stadium in the New Jersey Meadowlands, Labinski designed the ceilings two feet higher!

People planning on entering this career should integrate courses in sports studies into their school/college program, whenever possible, and maintain an ongoing interest in sports. In addition, they should gear course projects and field experiences toward sports facilities. The following organizations may be helpful to contact:

American Institute of Architects
1735 New York Avenue N.W.
Washington, DC 20006

American Design Drafting Association (ADDA)
P.O. Box 1799
Rockville, MD 20848-0799

National Society of Professional Engineers
1420 King Street
Alexandria, VA 22314

Sports Careers and the Internet

The growth of the Internet has expanded the horizons of available information about sports. This includes information related to employment possibilities as well as details of interest to practitioners in various fields.

For example, many professional organizations maintain Web sites through which you may access information. All you need to reach any such site is a computer with a modem and access to the Internet through a commercial on-line service or other provider of Internet services. By keying in a phrase such as "women in sports" or "Women's Sports Foundation," you can gain instant access to a wealth of information. The Web site for the Women's Sports Foundation includes the following details:

- background information about the organization including its goals, leadership, and members
- a description of four basic program areas: education (including a listing of publications and videotapes available through the Foundation); opportunities such as scholarships and grants; advocacy for change in policies, social patterns and laws affecting female sports and fitness participation; and programs honoring accomplishments of women in sports.

The site also includes membership information and the organization's telephone numbers and mailing address.

Information for coaches and other sports professionals can also be found on the Internet. For example, the *Journal of Basketball Studies* is an on-line magazine designed specifically for sharing information about effective coaching strategies.

Those seeking employment in sports-related areas can also use the Internet during the job search process. The Internet can be a great asset when it comes to looking for a job. Services such as "America's Job Bank" and other on-line job listings provide information about job openings around the country. You can browse through such listings and identify jobs of possible interest. Some listings allow you to search by job title or category. If you're interested in coaching, you might look under "education," "sports," or some related category. You can also limit searches to individual states, specific newspapers, or other characteristics.

Organizations for Women

Along with the growth in women's participation in sports, several organizations have focused their activities on women and sports. For example, the Women's Sports Foundation is a nonprofit organization that promotes the sports and fitness experience for women and girls. Established in 1974 by tennis great Billie Jean King and other female athletes, the Foundation provides scholarships, travel, and training grants for women and girls, paid internships related to sports careers, and other programs and services. Individuals are welcome to become members. For more information, contact the organization as follows:

Women's Sports Foundation
Eisenhower Park
East Meadow, NY 11554

Professional Wrestling Careers

One of the fastest growing sports in North America in the last 15 years has been professional wrestling.

A far cry from what you see on the mats in high school, college, or the Olympics, professional wrestling has strayed from the confines of strict, uniform rules to become more of an entertainment exhibition than a sport. Also unlike the more traditional forms, professional wrestling includes women as well as men, although the sexes do not normally compete against one another. Professional wrestlers typically wear flashy costumes, with one combatant taking the role of the hero and the other playing the part of the villain. The audience boisterously cheers the hero and jeers the villain. The match takes place in a padded, roped-off arena similar to a boxing ring. The opponents may cling to the ropes or even jump out of the ring during the match. Tag team matches, in which pairs of wrestlers take turns battling one another, also are popular.

A variety of jobs exist in the area related to professional wrestling, from ring announcer and manager to promoter and television commentator. Naturally, most of the attention is focused upon the combatants in the "squared circle."

The explosion of cable television and syndication has brought the colorful and exciting spectacle of professional wrestling into the living rooms of North America. Its widespread popularity has made household names of Hulk Hogan, Wendy Richter, Sycho Sid Sergeant Slaughter, The Road Warriors, Ric Flair, and others.

Wrestling Lifestyles

How can someone enter this career? King Kaluha is an example of a part-time wrestler. He suggested, "It helps to have a wrestling or martial arts (like karate) background. In addition, athletic experience and weight training are a must." Kaluha, who has bench-pressed over 400 pounds, has wrestled on the East Coast from Maine to Florida, usually in small facilities, arenas, and gymnasiums, on weekends or holidays.

King Kaluha said that wrestling is a great part-time job. During his first seven years of wrestling, he wrestled against some of the most famous wrestlers—Tonga Kid, David Sanmario, Rick Martel, Sergeant Slaughter, The Road Warriors, and others. He said, "I've always been an extrovert. The showmanship in this sport is perfect for me. There's not a lot of good wrestlers around. There's some big guys who can't wrestle or excite the crowd and some others close to retirement."

There are hundreds of professional wrestlers like Kaluha who work part-time. They may wrestle one to four days per week and lifts weights five or six days per week. People may pay them to appear at events like birthdays or car sales.

Offering the best in contemporary showmanship and wrestling skills is "Nature Boy" Ric Flair, the National Wrestling Alliance

(NWA) champion for many years. He wrestles in the United States, Canada, and other countries and is one of the best-paid athletes in North America. He learned from a former wrestling champion, Verne Gagne, who is now retired. Millions of people watch Flair's television performances, and from 500 to 20,000 people attend each of his live matches. Some weeks he travels only two miles, but other weeks he travels as far as Japan!

The life of a wrestler is very exciting, but it is also very hard work. Practicing takes a lot of time. Flair said, "I emphasize endurance training and weight training in my conditioning program. I even give my leisure time to athletic hobbies; I particularly like water sports.

"It's important to achieve athletically and academically," the world champion said. "The habits that you develop in school and college will help you compete in life and in the ring. In addition, read and study about topics that can enhance your athletic ability; for example, nutrition and weight training."

Not for Men Only

There exists a whole world of wrestling for women in the ring, not just as a manager, and it's growing.

Typical is the career of championship wrestling pro Heide Lee Morgan, originally from Elmer, New Jersey. As a young girl, she pursued gymnastics as a hobby while also enjoying dance, basketball, and softball. She said, "Gymnastics gave me the excellent agility so important in successful professional wrestling." In high school, she began weight training to shape and proportion her body. This resulted in her winning several bodybuilding championships, including becoming the two-time Greater Philadelphia Body Building Champion (women's teenage division).

Having developed an impressive sports body, she gained part-time employment in posing expositions, some of which were at wrestling events. Finally, after the encouragement of numerous people, she attended the Fabulous Moolah Wrestling School in Columbia, South Carolina.

Her life in the wrestling world really began when she attended matches of her father. He wrestled as "The Crazy Yankee" and as "Little Abner." When he participated in the latter role, she would precede him into the arena dressed as the cartoon character "Daisy Mae" and give daisies to the fans.

Upon completion of wrestling school, Morgan started slowly with matches on the East Coast. As she achieved success and the fans began to take notice, she moved up to wrestle for the American Wrestling Association (AWA) and the prestigious National Wrestling Alliance (NWA). Her success included being a member of the Ladies Professional Wrestling Association (LPWA) tag team champions. Heide's career has taken her to Japan, Italy, South America, Canada, and coast-to-coast in the United States. She stated, "One great fringe benefit is seeing the world and getting paid for it.

"Professional wrestling—as with life—causes you to make sacrifices if you want to be successful. However, one thing you should never sacrifice are your morals or values, or your reputation will be ruined," Morgan emphasized. She further added, "Women have been neglected and have not gotten their proper recognition in this business."

Getting Started

Professional wrestling today combines physical skills and showmanship. Therefore, future wrestlers need to develop good speaking skills.

Flair and Kaluha learned their profession as apprentices to other wrestlers. However, many future wrestlers will attend school to learn their skills. Wrestling schools teach young wrestlers special techniques of falling to prevent injury. The schools also teach different wrestling moves such as "body slamming," "suplexing," and "sunset flipping." There are many schools in the United States. Some of the well-known schools are listed at the end of this chapter.

"Opportunities exist for new wrestlers to rise to the top. But young people must remember that success requires developing a positive mental attitude and good habits," says Ric Flair. His words apply not only to the game of wrestling, but also to the game of life.

Pro wrestling fans interested in training for positions as ring announcers, managers, promoters, and related careers should contact one of the wrestling schools. Prospective employees should remember that, as with other jobs, beginners should start small—in this case, with independent regional promotions—and after gaining skill and experience, graduate to the "big time" (the major wrestling organizations). Salaries for major professional wrestlers are excellent; those for most related positions lag considerably behind the combatants. However, if you love "show business and rassling," this could be for you.

Some Wrestling Schools

Institute of Professional Wrestling
10 Stemmers Run Road
Essex, MD 21221

Ivan Koloff Wrestling School
P.O. Box 23360
Charlotte, NC 28227

School of Hard Knocks Wrestling School
3265 North E Street
San Bernardino, CA 92405

SkullKrushers Wrestling School
P.O. Box 6188
Gulf Breeze, FL 32561

Superstars Pro Wrestling Training Camp
21063 Cabot Boulevard
Hayward, CA 94545